Advance Praise

Each of us has a mother, so each of us has such a journey to make, like it or not. Thanks to this compelling diary, I feel better prepared for the journey ahead. This book is an intimate and heartfelt account of love and waging war with some of life's cruelties . . . so that life's beauty can shine through. And it does shine through. Wonderfully so.

> Donald Martin, Screenwriter
> Los Angeles, California

The journey taken by Charlene, her mother, and her family during the final months, weeks, and days of her mother's declining health and ultimate death truly touched my heart. And, as I begin to face the same issues with my own mother, I am grateful for the insight Charlene's journal has provided.

> Sandra F.
> Toronto, Ontario

If Mom's Not Dead by 9, I'm Leaving is a powerful testimony to love and letting go. Seeking spiritual illumination as she grapples with her mother's death, Roycht brings all of us into the deeper mystery of love and loss. A very moving read . . .

> Marianne Williamson

Reading this book . . . I lived a lot of it all over again, in my own way. I laughed and cried. . . . Please don't give up the time to be with a loved one at this time of their life.

> Mary Ellis, Caregiver
> Toledo, Ohio

Charlene takes you deeper each day. Her philosophical mind and spirituality become poetry! This is so emotional and touching. You're on this very private and special journey that's illuminating.

> Jo Raciti Forsberg, Improv Icon
> Chicago, Illinois

The journey you traveled with your mother and family and friends as your mother moved toward that good night is beautifully chronicled. As all journeys of faith proceed, one can put no real confidence in a preconceived road map. The bends and turns of the road are dictated by one's desire, unwilling as it often is, to be present to the moment—to the immense pain of traveling with a loved one who is diminishing physically. Your traveling with your mother and your reliance on God to be the navigator of the ship should definitely be shared with others who will inevitably travel similarly.

Brother Philip R. Smith, CSC, EdD
South Bend, Indiana

What a trip! With gut-wrenching honesty Charlene documents the incredible journey through the proverbial Valley of Death with her mother. A cancer survivor herself, Char is openly candid in the inclusive and painful account of her mother's death. . . . Thank you for your passion! Pax vobiscum.

Sharon Carlson, Actress, Talent Director for Out of the Box,
and voice teacher at Roosevelt University and Columbia College

This is . . . much more than a mere chronicle of events in the odyssey which covers a one-year vigil, as the author keeps watch over her mother's decline into the inevitable. Charlene skillfully uses the watch to explore fundamental issues of living relationships with self, fellow human beings, and God—with inimitable candor and honesty. Her punchy style spices the story, which will find moving echoes of similar experiences by all readers at some point in their lives. More significantly, the author shares caveats, admonitions, entreaties, and advice to help us lead richer lives in a more sane and peaceful world. As we read, we become more than spectators in the real-life drama which unfolds; truth becomes more engaging than imaginative fiction, till finally we are drawn into the story as participant-observers, albeit vicariously. As with the *Diary of Anne Frank*, the reader cannot simply walk away. And as with that classic, the genre is a potent vehicle for the purpose. All who read will be touched; many may change their perspectives on living for good.

Geoffrey Brown, Retired Associate Professor
of the University of the West Indies and writer
for the *Jamaica Daily Observer*

If Mom's Not Dead by 9, I'm Leaving

a journal about living, loving, dying

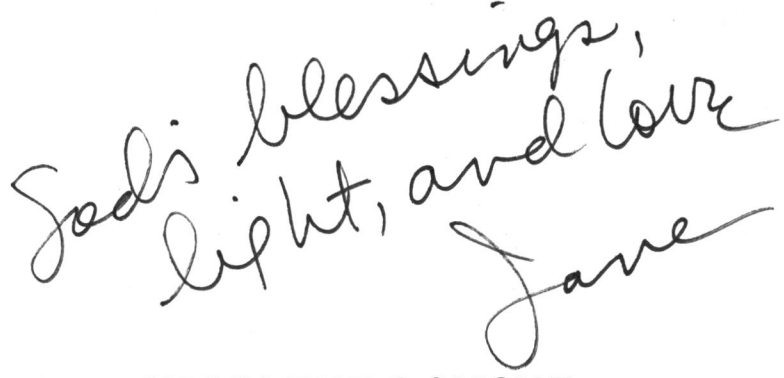

God's blessings, light, and love
Jane

CHARLENE ROYCHT

Charlene

Copyright © 2005 Charlene Roycht

All rights reserved. No part of this book may be reproduced or transmitted in any form or by any means, electronic or mechanical, including photocopying, recording, or by any information storage and retrieval system, without permission in writing from the publisher.

Published by Charoy Publishing
35 Courcelette Road
Scarborough, Ontario M1N 2S9
www.roycht.com

The Soul of Rumi, a new collection of ecstatic poems translated by Coleman Barks, © 2001. Permission in process with Harper Collins Publisher, Inc., New York, New York.

New and Selected Poems by Mary Oliver, © 1992. Permission in process with Beacon Press, Boston, Massachusetts.

Publisher's Cataloguing-in-Publication Data
Roycht, Charlene.
  If mom's not dead by 9, i'm leaving: a journal about living, loving, dying / Charlene Roycht. — Scarborough, Ontario : Charoy Publishing, 2005.

       p. ; cm.
       ISBN 0-9735963-0-9

  1. Mothers—Death. 2. Mothers—Death—Religious aspects.
3. Mothers and daughters. 4. Terminally ill parents—Family relationships.
5. Terminally ill—Psychology. 6. Bereavement—Psychological aspects.
7. Roycht, Catherine. 8. Roycht, Charlene. I. Title.

BF789.D4 R69 2005
155.9/37—dc22   CIP

Printed in Canada

10 9 8 7 6 5 4 3 2 1

            Cover and interior design by To The Point Solutions
                     www.tothepointsolutions.com

For Catherine Kerin Roycht, who was a remarkable woman.

Many thanks to God, Amma, and Marianne Williamson; for love, motivation, and inspiration.

Many thanks to the multitude of angels in my life, both up there and down here.

And, with total gratitude to my darling, Caroline.

INTRODUCTION

I have no idea why I started the diary. Just did. Almost from the get-go, it was about Mom's challenged health, my thoughts, my journey with Mom, and life in general. Spiritual growth. I wanted to encourage others to be with a parent. A loved one. To heal with them.

I've had a challenging time with my mom, over the years. I guess it started sometime after I told her that I was a happy lesbian. That was at age twenty-seven. Then, in my mid-forties, I owned my own being. My creativity. My truth. I had dabbled in that throughout life, but really owned it via the birth of my becoming a poet.

As I followed my truth, of being not only a poet, but also a creator, Mom and I really had a challenging time. She wanted me to stay in the same job, to work steadily and forever into pension and security. To not go "out of the box."

My spirit and passion were greater than a mother's wish. I did my own thing. So, we've had many years of uncomfortable silences, careful conversations, and unhappiness on both sides.

The back story will unfold, here and there. I wanted to concentrate on Mom. Her journey; right here and now. The feelings we have for each other, our growth, and my thoughts as they surfaced.

I'd have to honestly say Mom seemed to be unhappy for several years. When she started to not feel well, which was some time ago, she seemed sad. Mom's eighty-four. I'm sixty-two, as I write this.

Dad died in 1987, so Mom has had several years on her own. I don't think that was all that good. At a point, she became absorbed in her health challenges. Doctors became her hobby, medicines her unconscious passion. She loved her home in Sun City, Arizona. She was comfortable being alone.

This diary will mention my one and only sister, Donna, a lot. We're close and I love her. Her family, my partner, our lives; all here. My spiritual mentor, Marianne Williamson, plays a large role in my spiritual journey. Amma, the living saint from Kerela, India, plays an important role in my life, too. They both are instrumental in my journey with God.

This diary isn't easy to share. I don't mean to embarrass myself, or Mom, or my family and friends. If I did I'm sorry. It was not intended. Once you decide to share a journey, especially a diary, you record the truth. In the moment. All of it. Or what's the point? I share my diary with the hope of touching others in the same situation. Once you share that your mom is dying, you get endless tales from others who are going through this. The stories are mostly sad, with funny moments.

The mother-daughter thing . . . man, is that a thing! A journey unto itself. I'm not a mother; the daughter part was/is challenge enough! As I write these introductory remarks, I am shocked that Mom is still alive and attitudinally doing great. Our relationship is filling with love. Mom says she loves me, appreciates the time I spend with her, and enjoys my company! And, she's laughing . . . at the table she shares with a few others at Kingston Residence, in Sylvania, Ohio. She laughs, teases and stirs up "trouble." She truly is alive and, at least at mealtime, exudes energy.

You'll get to know mom and her state of health, which changes a fair bit. You'll get to know me and my sister. I guess what I want to say to you is heal . . . heal your relationship with your mom, your parents, your family—while they live. While you live.

Change. Forgive. Have peace in your family. Then try for your circle of friends, the community, and the world. One of my favorite Marianne quotes is, "Just as there is a so-called art of waging war, so there is an art of waging peace." I hope you are at peace, and that you'll bring peace to a loved one, to a dying one. Then, keep spreading it!

Enjoy the ride. Enjoy the read. God bless. Thanks.

(Written on November 21, 2002)

If Mom's Not Dead by 9, I'm Leaving

April 28, 2002

i'm writing this diary as i watch my mom, catherine roycht, go up and down with her health, i'm sure on her journey to death. she's having a hard time right now. her emphysema. her pneumonia. her labored breathing and that damn, hacking cough. it sounds so desperate. so tragic. it's not a pretty picture. not a great time. i go from lots of crying—to just sobbing—to praying full tilt boogie. i can't handle a lot of stress, nor should i, as i'm a cancer of the colon survivor and it's been about three years into my recovery. i live with looking over my shoulder, that "five year thing." if you don't get it back within a five-year period, perhaps you won't die from cancer of the colon. honestly, enough to drive one nuts. i could not handle mom's journey, or my own as a survivor, if i didn't pray. i pray my ass off. what's happened on my prayer journey . . . it's been amazing, it truly has. prayer calms me down, and i feel so close to god. however, i wish i could channel someone, "see" something. not yet. perhaps by the end of this book. i do a comedy act where i channel elizabeth, sister of lazarus. for short, "liz the lezzie." she's a member of the society of lesbian entities. has a mission to encourage and prepare more bodies to channel lesbian entities. it's a funny act. liz is in mothballs at the moment, as is a lot of my creativity. frankly, i have no energy. no extra energy, that is. i work, i pray, i participate in our home responsibilities, including the dogs and cat, and i go back and forth to toledo to see mom. to experience mom's journey. recording this is helpful. it's creative and i need that. it's healing, and that's working wonders for me. maybe it will help you. i do hope so. when mom is ill, it bothers me. last night, i thought she was dying. pneumonia. i think she came with it, from sun city, arizona. a major change for her. temperature change. just before we left sun city, we went to emergency, at the suggestion of our friend georgeta, who is knowledgeable in matters of medicine. damn if the diagnosis wasn't emphysema. since here, she's developed a cough, which has led to the pneumonia. and that's developed, big time. so here, in the hospital, there's that hacking cough when nothing comes up. and the struggle and gasping. and too, mom doesn't know how to breathe. a reminder for all of us. take deep breaths. this is so damn hard to watch. i see some lonely isolated tears at the edges of mom's eyes. that frightened facial expression. it's scary. i think this all started when mom felt a heaviness in her chest. called for help. eventually, she went to the hospital. to backtrack, upon arrival from sun city, mom and i stayed overnight at donna and ron's. the next day, in a very sad atmosphere, we got her ready to go to kingston residence, her new "home." can you believe that journey . . . at eighty-four . . . moving into a new residence, in an area you don't know, far away from your home of over twenty-five years and surrounded by people and a system you are totally unfamiliar with? mom. mom. mom. all old people leaving their homes. needing twenty-four hour care that a family or daughters and sons can't/won't provide. i imagine how sad they must be. how mom felt down deep, i'll never know. at that age, they don't talk of feelings. that generation never talked of feelings. think about it. it's so damn sad. so, here we are; mom in bed struggling to breathe, me on the side of the bed, hiding my tears and fears the best i can. i always wanted a picture-perfect death for mom. my sister and i would be with her. i know she loves us so much. mom would die in her sleep, calmly, peacefully. but damn, there's all this hacking and choking and panic attacks and old sad eyes and crying. my sister and i feeling helpless. sad and helpless. i have a heaviness in and around me. a dead energy that won't lift. i want to be or wanted it to be peaceful, relaxed and ever so loving with each word and touch. but i find myself being angry and short, demanding "mom, you've got to eat. mom, you've got to take your pills. mom, you've got to drink water. you've got to get fluids into your system." mom is yelling back, "i'm trying. i'm doing my best." i have to leave the room and cry. and just feel anger. there's no one to yell at, nothing to hit. no horn to blow, no body to give the finger to, or yell "fuck off" to. a good short cry. and back in the battle room. mom wasn't at kingston a week . . . not a week . . . and she's in the damn hospital, dying. i'm so pissed off. at god. at mom. isn't this so ridiculous? this is when i should pray. but i know it's ok to be pissed off with god. been there, done that. a lot. pissed off with mom, a bit much. get a grip, charlene. you are better than this. and i go for a walk. i find the chapel. i sit. i know, in silence, i'll feel better. i will empty my negativity so i can fill up with some positive feeling(s). i have flashbacks of so many trips to boswell hospital in sun city, to freedom plaza, the extended care unit connected with boswell. damn. now it's flower hospital. in toledo. oh god, i pray mom doesn't go. please. not so soon. give us a chance. for connection. for love. for forgiving and forgetting. oh god. please. what the hell am i writing about this for? i can just write a poem. this is too hard. too sad. oh god. i love my mom. give us some time! please give us some time. no, i'll change that god. please give my mom some time. some happy time. please. she is a good soul. she is. come on god. come on. enough already. i'm just a series of sighs. i have to cry. i will stop now. shared enough.

April 29, 2002

i'm thinking if i do this, i'll have to share some of our dysfunction. i think dysfunction is the norm and quite honestly, it's an awful term. we're all dysfunctional and from dysfunctional families. duh, we're in human form! to be above this, for christ's sake, we'd have to be shooting stars. i think my family is a bit above average. and so damn american. i love that. i do. i am a dual citizen. i've lived in canada more than half my life. i love both halves with all my heart. when i do visit mom, i immediately miss home and my life. i so appreciate the almost twenty-five years with caroline. our journey. our place of peace and love. our support for each other and the genuine feeling for each of us to be our chosen best. unfortunately, it's a health challenge for caroline now. she's on a waiting list with a top surgeon in toronto for a hip replacement. her pain, mostly arthritic and something from childhood . . . an injury that caroline can't remember . . . has caused her to use a cane, constantly. less and less mobility. it's hard to see. so i'm bookended by pain and challenge. thank god caroline's is not life threatening. but it's serious. when you love someone, it's so hard to see them in physical/pain/challenge. i'm in the hospital room and there are more friggin' bells going off. hospitals are busy places. i'm surprised any healing occurs. maybe it doesn't. maybe one overcomes trauma and goes home to heal. mother has had a few roommates at this hospital, they come and go as dis-ease becomes less. they all want to friggin' talk. leave my mom alone! leave me alone. peace. damn it. peace. mother is resting. i hope this crisis is over. her breathing is getting less labored. hope we've turned a corner. mom's most likely to be transferred to lake park, the extended care facility connected with this hospital. that's good. donna is part owner of great lakes medical review. they monitor patients on long-term care and medicare. donna is at lake park a lot. that'd be good for mom. mom's been poked, prodded, given lots of oxygen treatments, is on oxygen, and has had some damn good nursing care. i feel like i've been in a dream. a bad dream. the dream started when mom fell again in her home in sun city. crawled to the phone. called her neighbor, our family friend now, daphne. daph came over, mom was on the floor. daph called cathy and ralph. they called the paramedics. mom broke her hip. this was this past february. mom's fallen before. she's not told us about all of the falls. but donna and i agreed, "one more mom, and that's it. you can't live alone." and this one, the broken hip fall, was it. mom's lived alone since dad died. that's about fifteen years ago. spent many years, after that, helping to feed the poor with the st. vincent de paul society. even as her health failed, she kept volunteering. when her efforts for feeding the poor were "not needed" anymore, at the dining room in the town of surprise, arizona, i know her heart was broken. i don't know what happened, exactly. after that, she still helped with the odd thing for st. vincent de paul, but it was too quiet. she had so little to do. nowhere to go. nowhere to put her energy. she sat at home and started to wither away. donna and ron in toledo, me in toronto. well, nick, donna's son, is in the phoenix area. he had been stellar. daily phone calls, weekly cleans, errands. caring. but mom did wither away. she started to not eat right. i don't think she handled her medicine well. she started to fall. in the autumn of 2001. we didn't know about all of them right away. we caught up. and mom just couldn't be left alone any longer. donna and ron started a search in their area and hit upon kingston residence. it's assisted living plus. they were sold on the plus. reluctantly, mom finally agreed to come to the toledo area, until donna retired in september 2002. then go back. they'd all work out something. and that was the deal. as i sit here, i wonder if mom's going back in a box. damn. this is so sad. she wasn't here but one week. can you believe it? i feel like i just want to watch mom breathe. and sleep. and pray silently. i do want her to live. and feel better. damn. please, god. please.

May 1, 2002

why am i shouting "you go, girl!" . . . but i am. mom's on a pill strike! except for tylenol . . . she's refusing all pills. has had it! what a gal. that's my mom. go girl! spunky, stubborn. so proud. i'm so proud. i can't blame her. she's been nauseous for the last two days. she takes a shit load of pills . . . something like twenty, in a day . . . that's quite a few. they are just so damn hard to swallow, to digest. she's just off the near-death struggle, wasn't eating that much—too damn sick—and they'd force her to take these mothers. she could hardly get them down, then she'd upchuck. so today, mom said, "that's it, no more pills!" i love it. taking charge. a lesson here, folks. i'm happy for her; proud of her. it's not going to kill her. i think after a day or so . . . her system calming down, perhaps with some food in her, slowly, she'll start to feel better. when you're sick, you're sick! christ. let's review the pill list and get rid of some. honestly, a pill for every damn thing you can imagine. i think old people take too many pills. hell, i even take too many pills; vitamins, etc. it's a shame, isn't it? mom is a worry, though. i didn't sleep last night. well, waking up at 4:10 a.m. isn't a good sleep. i'm thinking about my life, my choices, my dreams. things i want to do. i'm a co-active personal coach now, not certified, but don't think i'll go for certification. for what i'm doing and how, i don't think certification matters. we'll see. thinking about my "concentration" in coaching. it's for sure "on purpose" . . . what's a person's purpose . . . in life? so important to explore that, to unearth it for one's self. i can do that kind of coaching in a three hour session. discover one's life purpose. that's so good. we should all know our reason for living. live our passion. be aware of our gifts and live them. i just thought about that upon waking. i'm so excited. then, somehow, i was thinking of the vagina monologues and how brilliant eve ensler is. i don't know the woman, but my god; brilliant, visionary, generous, responsible. pretty powerful. would love to meet her. at one of our training sessions, i unearthed my life purpose statement: i am a spirit wanderer ringing the bell of life. it's so me. i am a spirit. i love the freedom of wander and wonder. i am ringing my bell of life in all its glory; i am a natural encourager of others to ring their own bells. it's so right on for me. i will give back; like eve. i do that, just a bit now. i'm very supportive of my friends, emotionally. am there for them. that's good. important. with the coaching, i can be there more fully. even for mom, i can explore our relationship in different ways now. i have more tools. i need to do that with mom. it's been a bit of a struggle here and there for us. mom doesn't quite "get me." lots of people don't, really. i'm a dragon, an aries, i am fire. i'm bright a lot. i'm hot. lots of logs on my fire, constantly. sometimes it wears me out. i can simmer, too. i need to simmer a bit more methodically with mom, now. she's tender. well, i am, too. oh hell, we all are. i think life is about hearing our own music, and dancing. i've done that, easily. that's a gift. mom's a dancer . . . she sewed, baked, she kept our home very clean and was organized. she worked many jobs to make extra money for our education, she was a superb waitress and hostess, she was a tease and a flirt. lots of personality. when mom and dad retired, she got involved in the church and the-at the time-yugoslavian club in sun city. our heritage. even held different offices at various times, including president! she volunteered feeding the poor, through st. vincent de paul, for years. so, she's a dancer. was a good dancer. there's a quote on the wall coming into lake park that says "love is the act of sensing or hearing the special music in another's spirit—and in those times when they forget their song—we sing the words back to them. again." in a way, that's the care system, isn't it? people losing a bit of their pizazz because they don't feel well and health care workers, families, and friends help them mend . . . through love. we sing the song back to them. live. love. feel better. laugh again. oh god, i hope mom feels good again, soon. i hate seeing her sick. god bless you, the reader. if you're not singing to someone, get your butt in gear. there is always someone who needs the song. don't know how to sing? take lessons! god bless you. god bless us all.

May 6, 2002

i'm writing while eating high-fiber crackers and sipping cold white wine. i feel good; mom is much better. i cannot believe the journey she's been on since falling and breaking her hip on february 2nd. donna and i went out to arizona, can't remember the dates. then donna, ron, and i went back for two more weeks, packed up mom, brought her back to toledo. i believe we traveled from arizona to ohio on april 9th. donna and ron, with some help from nancy, decorated mom's kingston room. mom was there one week and then came down with pneumonia. i got called, drove fast from toronto, where i live. the following two weeks were hospital and extended care. it's mother's day this sunday. i went to warren, michigan, last sunday, to hear marianne williamson speak at renaissance unity. i talked to marianne after the service, briefly. she had an assistant give me her tape on death and dying. it has meant so much to me. i've helped my friend sandra with the death of a friend. i helped another friend, in challenge. "pay it forward." if you've not seen that movie, it's worth your time. really, it is. not only for the concept . . . but also for helen hunt, kevin spacey and the kid. actually, now that i'm thinking about it, i loved that movie. walking my dogs this week, in the beaches area, i've discovered a few others with mom problems; ill heath, decisions to make, stressed out by the current situation. being sixty-two, i find others near and around my age are very often in the same boat. lynn and barb have stories. lynn's mom is not well at all, barb and her mom never healed. didn't we have fun joking about "the real mother's day cards they should write." very sacrilegious. funny. mean. honest. embarrassing. went to toronto's religious science church this sunday with michael, rita's mentally challenged brother visiting from florida. what a good church that is. it's always such a great experience being with michael; he puts me in the now and sure simplifies one's view of the world. we need more experiences like that. when i review my life, who and what i have in it, including mom, i'm so grateful. i am. i have a loving sister, brother-in-law, partner, two fabulous dogs, and one fabulous cat, wonderful friends, good and loving family. i live in a terrific city and in a wonderful and beautiful community right by lake ontario. i've good energy . . . a loving heart. jesus. i'm blessed. i'm grateful. i'm happy. aren't i lucky! oh yeah, i'm financially challenged, but in the long run, that's minor. i'm trading time for money, connection for money, deepening my spirit and soul. i always put my time to good use. i constantly work on my connection with god. i know there is one; just can't quite explain "it." heaven? hell? what happens when we die? trust something ok does happen, don't know what. ok by me. i just saw "contact" last night, again, on tv. that was an interesting movie. about faith, trust, science, reality, mystery. that's all about god, isn't it? i think that's why i love marianne williamson so much; she can put profound thoughts into simple words. her lectures are often based on a course in miracles; a psychological thought process based on love. remarkable material. i think one thing that makes me happy is my yearning for a deeper connection with god; which translates into a yearning for a deeper relationship with mom. now that she's here, what an opportunity for me. oh boy, i hate that mom is sick right off the bat. hopefully, when she recovers, we can have some good mother-daughter time. grow a bit. heal a bit. our conversations have been limited over the years; weather, work. emotionally mom gave up on me many years ago; when i cheated on caroline. caroline and i broke up; miraculously stayed together, but changed our relationship. i started to have many girlfriends. some at the same time! oh god, i was a mess. my personal process and progress was messy, at times embarrassing. but i persevered with therapy, self-help gurus, spiritual practice and a burning desire to become a better, well-balanced person. i often approached mom about expanding the boundaries of our conversations, but she'd have no part of my version of improving mentally, psychologically, emotionally. "let's not go there" was a constant wall. hopefully, now that she's captive, i can tear down the wall. mom, hang on. it's going to be a bumpy ride. love you. get better mom. please, get better.

May 9, 2002

i was in anxiety yesterday. i'm discovering i'm an emotional eater. i go between the conscious-unconscious process about mother dying. somewhere in between i need to fill up with mother's love. yearn for it. simple kindness, a look, a question about me, about the inner me; that kind of love. i did not stop eating yesterday. emotional eating. and yes, emotional drinking. i cry; every now and then it just comes, just cry and cry. the bucket syndrome. i had two quick chats with mom; calling to say hi and i miss you, mom, love you. she's not a phone girl. i wish there were more to say on the phone. when i came out as a lesbian it was on paper, a letter. she was in arizona, i was in toronto. i really thought she knew; there seemed, to me, to be hints throughout the years. i finally felt comfortable with confirming it. prior to caroline, i always needed excitement, newness, challenge. an aries, an airhead, a dragon, a fire that hated to simmer and go out. craved attention, constantly. when I fell in love with caroline, i wanted mom to know me, us. mom had an extremely hard time with my declaration but, upon meeting caroline, loved her, us. when caroline and i split, mom disowned my lesbian lifestyle. didn't want to hear about anyone, about my falling in love, out of love, my process. caroline and i somehow worked through my madness and wound up living together. together for i think, mmm, almost twenty-five years, now. we're, let's see, non-monogamous, interdependent, loving, caring, lifetime partners. as we put it, we'll grow old together, bury each other. lovers come and go, not often, but when they do, they have to fit into our family, our home. somewhere along the path, we arrived at the knowledge we never wanted to live with our lovers. we love our home, as is. it's worked for us. mom felt dad would "never get it, or me" and therefore i never shared it with him. i want mom to know the magnificent me, damn it. i've got work to do, to get there. i don't know what your problems are, but face them, deal with them. get a grip. get help, if you need it. really, they . . . your mom or dad, did their best. get on with it. takes time, effort, process. i really hope you look into that relationship; and embrace it. have it end in peace, if possible. that's my goal. i intend to embrace my mom. and me. i arrived at this point, after many years of therapy, spiritual experiences, of learning to love myself. my god, that's worth all the time, money, pain, digging, shit, and tears. it's a commitment to the process. now, this time with mom, actual time with her, is frosting on the cake. let's face it, if the frosting isn't good, the cake loses something too. mom openly says "love you" to me . . . to donna. she even says she'll miss me when i hit the road to toronto. it's incredible. i think being alone for so many years in arizona, it was too lonely for mom. i can't tell you how it makes me feel when she says those things. so filled. so happy. you just can't buy that kind of feeling. you can't. she even is sharing how much she's appreciating donna and me taking care of her; seeing her, seeing to her every need. it brings tears to my eyes. this is such a healing process for me. i don't think mom feels it the same way i do. she'll never talk about feelings; she just doesn't get it when i want to have that kind of conversation. i laugh. that generation was just not built that way. donna and i see things so differently, too. she never had therapy. i'll ask donna about childhood things and honestly, it's two different experiences. just the two of us; two and half years apart. donna older. she's fem; i'm lesbo. i was a tomboy;

give me the guns, the trucks. oh man, i laugh. now i'm so anti-gun. laugh harder. god bless differences. oh god, me and a dress . . . even in childhood . . . oh god, disaster. i hated dresses. i remember once, i was to wear a dress to grandma's on sunday, and i wouldn't. damn if mom stayed home with me, while i cried and cried. it was fun at grandma's, all the cousins played dress up and did plays, using the dirty clothes in the hamper! i had battles with dresses and dress codes. especially mom's. so there's been a journey for mom and me. i was different. mom did her best. the love, as i wanted it, with who i was, wasn't there. so i am now loving the words when spoken, the looks, the reaching out of a hand, the smiles that are beginning to happen. my mom has been mean. cold. short. she can and did "disappear." could just be nonexistent in a room. it was awful. i had many a bad visit, on my own, to her house. the first day or two great, and then that cold, stone-like, miserable, unknown would be present. my guess, many things; not much to say, obligation being met, interfering with mom's non-routine and routine, just interfering. she so started to love being by herself. can't tell you how many times i would just bawl. cry. sob. i remember going to the pet cemetery in sun city, a lot, just crying. it was a peaceful place to be. boy, we had some miserable times. just couldn't communicate. mom's been this way with donna and ron, too. even to neighbors and friends. she hates intrusion. loves her routines. i'm beginning to understand my mom. just beginning. i can only imagine if she were to write a diary. holy shit. that would be something to read. she gets hurt easily. will go mute. won't share. and store, just stores that negative energy. that is so unhealthy. perhaps that's why she's ill; with so many little things that make it a big thing. age, depression, loneliness, arthritis, everything—everything starting to fail, and leaving her home. i can't imagine leaving one's home. one's stuff. all that is familiar. christ. i admire my mom. i'm actually proud of her. just love her. i don't want her to suffer. please god, i hope she's not on that list. all i can say, is god, i'm so grateful mom is with us. that donna and ron are close by and so generous. that i'm a five-hour drive away. that i work in an industry where i can come and go. that caroline is so understanding. my god, it's good. this journey, with mom, is good. i love you mom, so much. god bless. i'm enjoying the communication. i am. just get better!

May 13, 2002

here with mom at lake park; most likely last full day here; awaiting discharge orders to return to kingston—her assisted living apartment near by. i think it's great. her own space once again. she's only been there six days since we arrived in toledo. i've prayed for mom to be healthy, for her to be able to have some joy, some fun, some days/months . . . or longer . . . of feeling better. maybe my prayers will be answered. i hope. i hope. i'm trying to live in the present moment. the now. for today, it's good. i am there. i feel good. it feels good. mom's eating very well. should check with donna or the nurse; wonder if this is a natural appetite or the megace? actually mom's eating like a horse. she's a tiny person. i bet she weighs . . . 115 pounds. she's 5' 2". little. she's starting to bulge. ah, who cares. she says she doesn't sleep well at night. she's always said that. today she said she woke up at 1:00 a.m. and never went back to sleep. then she's so tired during the day. we've discussed protective undergarments. well, actually she listened in on a conversation that the nurse, roomie bess, and i were having. she listened. didn't say a word. she's been wearing diapers . . . well, protective garments as they are now called. it is degrading. the transition into them; it's degrading. i guess we'll all be there. i'm pretty sure she'll be better off with them from now on. when she has to go, there just isn't the time or the ability to get to the bathroom fast enough. mom has no time from feeling to release. the protective garments are good protection. now, disposable. they've come a long way, baby. she's been wearing too bulky, too large a diaper. the nursing assistant found a smaller size. it's better. i'll shop around and see if i can't get a supply of them for mom. at kingston, each person wears a "call bracelet." i don't know if mom uses hers often enough. if at all. think about it; an old lady, with a walker, schlepping to the bathroom, having to go, big bulky diaper on, pees in the diaper. tries to change herself. i can't see it. it's dangerous. it's disastrous. this is a fall waiting to happen or permanent rash from urine. oh, this aging. not pretty. i'm overly protective of mom. i worry. oh god, i worry. the next fall could mean permanent wheelchair. you see how in the now i am. damn, this is hard. i so easily go to a darker possibility with mom. a course in miracles and marianne williamson are helping me. ah, marianne. she's so well read, so knowledgeable about the process of trying to be the best and most loving we can be. my life is so much better with her books, tapes, lectures at renaissance unity in warren, michigan. honestly, i'm a better person because of her, that church. all of it. better with mom. marianne really motivates me. it's not so much marianne; it's how marianne helps me connect with god. that's really it. god is really the saving grace. so many people seem to be afraid of admitting their closeness with god. why's that? off on a tangent. back to mom and possible disaster in the future. mom is sleeping; i'm watching cnn, with the sound off, bess has gone to therapy. mom will go at two. this room is so crowded. mom's oxygen tank (big), her wheelchair, her walker, her commode (big), her bedside table, two chests of drawers and her twin bed. then there's bess and her stuff. trust me, it's a bloody small room. mom's been in front of the one window, which is great. bess will take over mom's bed when we go. such a nice view; trees, sky, space. we can't see the large pond that lake park and the accompanying hospital has. but it's huge, with all kinds of water fowl. a lovely "campus." i sit here and feel blessed to have time with mom, time with my sister, "sharing the load." it's a lot. i can't believe how emptying mom's commode or wiping mom's behind is "just a thing now." it's such a challenge for mom to go to the bathroom; with pulling her slacks down and undoing the diaper. she's too weak to stand up on her own, most of the time. it's so bloody sad. it's work. for all involved. just the freakin' bathroom. but she is getting stronger. that's good. reality check; she has emphysema and when i hear that congestive cough—it's such a horrible sound—i know my face just crunches up. at kingston, she'll get assistance with dressing in the morning, go to breakfast, then rest in the room. go to lunch. rest in the room. some tv. go to dinner. rest in the room. some tv. get assistance with her pj's and getting the bed ready. that'll be her life; except for our visits and outings. oh god, we push and push about her going to activities; which kingston has so much of. but, she's just not an activity gal. donna or donna and ron will take her out. she'll get her hair done at kingston. she gets her nails done there. her big outing will be sunday dinners at donna and ron's with other family. sometimes donna and ron's neighbors and good friends jim and sandy join in. that's good. donna drops in on mom every day. if not twice a day. that's why it's so good mom's here. now if she'll only get healthy to enjoy it all. nancy (donna's daughter) and her daughter, elizabeth, are here; mom enjoys them. mom knows most of ron's family. ron's brother dick and his wife, lola, come around. and mom was just beginning to bond with the kingston staff. so i think it's going to be all right. i'm back and forth from toronto every two or three weeks. i phone almost daily or every other day . . . never more than three days pass. so mom's got a good shot at being—i'll go out on a limb and say—happy. happy? i hope happy. at least surrounded by loving people. i look at mom and just smile. she's really a remarkable woman. strong in so many ways, including headstrong. god i love her. i hope mom will talk to me about feelings one day. i hope. enough for today.

May 14, 2002

tuesday at kingston in mom's small apartment; it's so hot in here. i'd be stripping down to bare necessities or no necessities, but it's mom's first day back. don't want to upset her, in any way. i'm sure the nursing director will be dropping by; she knows we're back. as you may recall mom wasn't here a week and the pneumonia hit. still has that ugly hacking full phlegm cough. a constant reminder of the emphysema. mom smoked many years. quit cold turkey in arizona a few years ago but smoked far too many years. no smoking . . . readers. no smoking! emphysema is ugly. painful. thank god mom does not need oxygen, at this point. i just reviewed mom's discharge papers from lake park; the extended care we just left. more than twenty friggin' pills, puffs, liquids. she takes too many. just too many. christ, no one can be that ill. i'll list them at the end of this entry. we must bloody well get her off of some of these. she was sleeping, but got up to go to the bathroom. she'll need a lot of assistance. she had bowel stains in her undergarment, so we changed that. i bought her depends refasten underwear, super, for an experiment in overnight protection. my god, there are so many choices. pads with belts (remember the ol' kotex), which seemed a bit too much. so many briefs, sizes, protection descriptions. almost need a degree to buy the right kind. i really liked the disposable brief, but they only had regular protection. thought it best to go with the super. we'll see. i think we'll be able to sort out protection. this is quite a serious challenge. a difficult transition. i wouldn't say mom is incontinent. i find that a rather removed word from the actual problem. continent or incontinent? it's a strange word. the reality: such a personal human challenge. a delicate one. mom is in question. we are in "gray." have yet to see an internist about mom's bladder, which was on the books before pneumonia took us for a ride. mom's challenge—sleeping soundly through the night, having the constant bathroom challenge. feeling a pee coming on and bingo. no time for travel. she's just so tired. so tired. we ate lunch with two wonderful people today; brenda, eighty-three, mother of seven, woman of color, american. and richard, eighty-two, two months after his open heart surgery. both delightful, talkative, interesting. really nice. mom was totally silent except for a few loud belches; and she never says excuse me. also a few loud coughs, for a duration of time, with no covering of the mouth. i had to say, "mom, cover your mouth, please" as kindly as i could. her manners drive me nuts. but then, a few of the other people act similarly. donna will be by later, after work. i'll stay until tomorrow after lunch, just keeping mom company. i try to see it, feel it, from mom's point of view. being here in toledo, at kingston, all of it so new . . . it's very challenging. i'm sure she feels quite alone. she may feel a bit more social in a day or two. but that's my aries, pushy bitch idea. why would it go so quickly? mom is sensitive. oh, i can't stand my thinking sometimes. i just couldn't leave her as soon as she moved in. aging is sensitive! to the reader, i plead with you; be sensitive with your parent(s) in this situation. remember all they gave to you. i hope i get mom to talk a bit about her feelings. eventually. today i know would be pushing it. very quiet. she's feeling something; but only god knows. if i did any digging it would create isolation. sometimes there is a lengthy punishment that goes with probing. i'll just try to be as kind and considerate as i can be. i do my own thing in her quietness: write, read, listen to tapes.

sometimes watch tv with no sound. at times, mom likes it absolutely quiet. i'm good with time; never at a loss for things to do. can always pray, meditate, just be. i always have a few cards to write; friends all over the world and mom's friends in sun city. they have been worried. mom was a real presence in the neighborhood, at church and at st. vincent de paul. unfortunately, she's not a good phone person, which is too bad. basically she's unavailable as she's not happy with her handwriting either. christ, it's hot in here. i'm glad i'm here. i do love my mom. i feel sad. this is sad. i know mom misses arizona so much. misses home. i miss home. i love my home, my life. time. time is so bloody important, isn't it? time to have to do what's good, what's right, what's important. god i miss my life; driving, coaching, the dogs, the cat, caroline. i'm thinking of my "on purpose" coaching. we should all know or dig for the answer as to our purpose for being here. i love who i am; a spirit wanderer ringing the bell of life. that's me. i love the visual. i sure want everyone to see their glass half full. get on with their gifts and passion. a lot of people are dead. what a shame. life is damn rich every moment. i never got death, while living. sometimes i feel guilty about not doing enough with my twenty-four hours each day. folks, we've got twenty-four each day. how divine. hope you're living yours. and duh, get a coach! right now, i'm challenged with time as i don't have enough for me. but i'm happy to have so much with and for mom. i really am grateful. i'll get to everything else. i will. now, it's mom time. travel time. family time. in mom's kingston bulletin, this past month, there was quite the quote by h. carter: "a wise woman once said to me . . . there are only two lasting bequests we can hope to give our children. one of these is roots; the other wings." my god, isn't that lovely? i am so grateful mom gave me roots. mom and dad. i feel my roots, i do. and wings; oui, wings i got. i'm a flyer. mom and dad; you did good. i know my constant thing is "i never got the love i wanted." duh. they couldn't give it. i'll just get over it one day. pretty well over it now. at one point . . . and i can't remember when . . . mom said, "all i know is i'll get back to arizona." that is definitely a possibility. donna is retiring, ron's retired. they could go back and live there; but not with mom. it would kill donna. mom would need too much care. no living dogs, either. ah, maybe mom could get over that. then too, for help, hired help? lots to think about. mom loves arizona, her home. why shouldn't she? fantastic state, great home. oh mom, i pray you'll get back. you all can get a plan together that works. you do deserve happiness till your dying day, mom. and please god, may she live a long, healthy life! well, as healthy as can be. enough of thoughts on paper for today. time to be with my mama. god bless everyone. hope you are being good to your parent(s)!

Mom's Meds

norvasc—blood pressure medicine, also evens out the heart beat

caltrate—calcium supplement

muro eye drops—relieves dry eyes

colace—relieves constipation

protonix interchanged with prilosec—prevention of stomach acid and ulcers

prednisone—steroid to help her breathe

synthroid—for slow-acting thyroid

premarin—controls hot flashes

miacalcin—nasal spray . . . added calcium to her system

prevacid— interchanged with other meds to help prevent stomach ulcers. did not take all at the same time

lasix—diuretic, kept body swelling down

pletal—promoted blood circulation in mom's legs

aerobid inhaler—to help breathing (when on the aerosols four times a day, did not use)

cellrolid aerosol with adapter—used this with the oxygen breathing machine. the meds were albuterol and ipratroium bromide (duo neb)

zocor—for high cholesterol

zoloft—antidepressant

megace—to promote appetite

xanax—to reduce anxiety

robitussin—cough suppressant

calcium carbonate—calcium supplement

iron

lipitor—for high cholesterol. interchanged with zocor

the puff type aerosols could be used with the adapter as well as the one med—could have been combivent

potassium chloride

zaroxolyn—reduce edema

    Note: I did my best to get this all right.

May 16, 2002

in toronto. sitting in my car, waiting for our dog casey to dry, after a bath at bark and wag, here on broadview avenue. this is good. anytime to write is good. i do want to be disciplined about writing the diary. a bit challenging. it's coming, though. i walked the dogs, before the rain came, went for a swim, which is so good for my body, ran a few errands and then home. e-mails, phone calls, a caroline catch up as she's home today. god bless home. we decide to go out for lunch before i take casey to bark and wag. a good way to catch up. caroline's got lots to do; has to work on a presentation . . . some part of her jungian workshop over the weekend. and so it goes; life. not necessarily in the fast lane either. just life. usually when i get home, i cry or am prone to crying about mom. it's worry, it's knowing anything, any kind of news, is a phone call away. mom said to me, sometime before i left, "i've got to move, and push myself. i know that." now i remember, she said it at breakfast yesterday. i arrived and she still was in the dining room with another resident, charlotte. a stroke victim in a wheelchair. i was so happy to see mom talking with someone! mom had diarrhea yesterday; she had diarrhea when she moved in the first time. i don't like that. i hate it but wasn't so grossed out this time. the throw away briefs are great; especially with the diarrhea. they really helped. wiping up the mess; washing out the slacks; it's all so gross. poor mom. mom was concerned with the cost of the throwaways . . . i laugh. mom is so money wise. and tight. a good teacher that way. really. i didn't think they were that expensive. whatever they were—worth every penny. when i worry, i pick my nails. always have been a nail biter. during this intense time i make sure i get manicures. i should get a reduced price for my stubs, but it's a good practice for me. honor my stubs and encourage me to keep them out of my mouth. mom always keeps her nails so nice. she yells at me whenever i'm into a bite on mine. well, it might be time to check on casey. i have a feeling she'll be done. more to come. i'm back; casey's not done yet. got the ol' shaking the head no from donna, when i peeked in the window. remembering that mom and i ate lunch with charlotte before i left. i think mom wants a connection with her; that is so great. her first friend at kingston. charlotte is paralyzed on one side; partial use of one hand, arm. doing pretty damn good given her physical challenge. auto-motorized chair. amazing. inspiring. perhaps mom will be inspired. when i look at the kingston crowd, many seem so challenged. but god bless them. they move, talk, visit. mealtimes are the real social times. there are also a lot of activities. i guess you are into those or not. mom is not. i usually have to take a moment once i'm in my car, leaving kingston. it's the fragility of old age that gets me. the potential downhill slide that can be so fast. it's so damn sad. and my mom is on that slide. i think that's why i cry a lot. it's just damn sad. i honor the people who choose to work in health care. i find them remarkable. it just seems so challenging. seemed like everyone was going to listen to accordion music after lunch. the table encouraged mom to go. surprise. we went! well, my mom thought it was the worst accordion music in the world. we're yugoslavian; frankie yankovic devotees. mom was almost embarrassing in her dislike of this particular accordion guy. i laughed. mom has no patience. and guess what? i'm just like her. i have none, either. so we split after a short time. back up in mom's room. she was happy. she's been a loner in arizona; i think she'll be doing the same here.

meal socializer. that's ok. i don't know if my mom is lonely. i don't think she'll admit that. i like being alone. this is scary. i'm so much like my mom. echt. donna is too. echt. donna is a doting grandmother. nancy has elizabeth, now seven. sharon and mike have heather, about eight, daniel about five and erin about three. nick has no kids. nick is in phoenix; originally came to the area to work and be near grandma. he's been good to her! but, back to donna; she loves when she does get time to herself, which is rare. probably could be a bit of a loner. oh mom. god bless you, girl. i can't believe how donna and i have our parents' traits. now i'm seeing it. echt. mom has been so generous to donna and me. and her grandkids. and their kids. i'm so appreciative, about so many things. my health for sure. that's number one. i'm three years and eight months post cancer of the colon. still a bit tired, if you can believe it. strength coming, slowly. can't seem to hit any real rhythm since being ill and now with mom so challenged, don't know what's up. perhaps we'll get into a bit of a pattern. oh mom. i hope you'll be healthy. and happy. enjoy kingston. your family. love you, mom. i do so love you. well, i'd better go get the hound dog. enough for this day. god bless you, mom.

May 20, 2002

mom fell, again. this past friday. donna told me saturday. mom has always been so protective of me regarding anything that happens to her; "don't tell charlene. she'll get too upset." donna has always listened to mom regarding this. it bugs the shit out of me. yes, i know i react with so much emotion but . . . duh . . . i have a right to know. i've been working on mother and donna regarding their pact. but this time, when donna found out, she told me. i guess mom told donna well after the fall! donna raised holy hell at kingston. she should have been notified. there was some miscommunication. i can't remember all the details. i can't remember if i wrote about this. it all becomes a blur. i worry. i do. constantly. i was feeling a poem today, at one point. that's how they come to me . . . either a line, the whole thing, or a feeling about the whole thing. it started with "a part of me." it went something like "a part of me is waiting for the next terrorist attack. a part of me is waiting for mom to die. a part of me thinks i might die before mama." i've been feeling that the last few days; since i went to the doctor and found out i have extensive degenerative disk problems. funny how your mind can fast forward. after september 11th, i feel so changed. a whole part of me has not recovered yet. i keep waiting . . . it's a bummer. and then there's mom; always a phone call away from what? what? "she's not as good as she looks." that's the current mantra from donna and the doctor. now this damn disc thing. i know i'll be fine. it's like the cancer of the colon. you're dealt a card. then god sees what will you do with this. i'm ok with whatever i'm dealt. i'm truly ok. i have such a desire to live and live fully, totally. i do get down. mom has me down today. but i'll work on getting up. usually a movie does it. i drive in the film/tv industry. i'm in transport. i love having a part in making movies. i love movies. always have. i love going alone, or with friends; just get me to a movie, or rent a dvd or video. always comforting. so much in my head today. poetry idea. marketing ideas. deck of poems. in a box, like a deck of cards. fifty-two of them. mine, of course. not bad, charlene. i can do that. another coaching idea; "in-significance." it would be the theme of a certain coaching session, to find what's important to you. significant in and for you. how one honors that. i knew i was a natural coach once i took the training. love coaching; love my clients. oh, i love so many things. poetry. reading poems. writing them. i'll grow old with loving poetry. i know that. lately i've just felt the need to write. i'm so happy to record mom's journey. i'll connect with an old friend—another poet—this week. we'll continue our poetry exchange; we call and read to each other. time limit or poem limit. works well. i'll have to read what i'm writing about mom. no new poetry. that'll work for me. impetus to keep writing, too. mom went to donna's on sunday. i like when that happens. i like that a lot. mike and sharon are off to germany, with the kids, for three years. they leave next tuesday. mike's an army man. i'm so glad mom had a little time with them. now mom just has nancy and elizabeth close by; as far as a grandchild and great grandchild. nancy is so much fun and high energy. elizabeth is sweet. so mom's family circle is a bit smaller, but still mighty. that's it for today. mom, oh god, mom. please be careful. please! use that damn call bracelet! get assistance. you're in assisted living! duh. love you mom. i do. but damn, be careful!

May 22, 2002

rima's mother died. i saw her this morning while walking sammie and casey. i felt so sad. she said it was beautiful; so many things about it of beauty. the family was with her. then she said a curious thing: "we prepare, we know, but i just can't get used to the possibility of getting used to living without her." it was said in the most beautiful and respectful manner. for some reason, i just cried and cried when i got in my car. cried about mom. some days i just want to relocate so i can be nearer to her. of course, i can't, but i'd love to. i'm too far. five hours away is too far. caroline, her hip, our home, my needing to work . . . all prohibit this actuality. it's in my heart, mom. it's in my heart. oui. for some extra money. i'm still at the park, writing. don't know why. i'll spend the day with michael. i'm one of the "pals" hired to keep him company and care for him while rita and ingrid work. it's such an eye opener . . . spending time with someone mentally challenged. other than myself, that is. michael is sweet, caring, sensitive; he's innocence. he'll shoot baskets; can do this for an extended period of time. i'm thinking about rima's mom; that pain is so transferable. then i think of my dear friend cj who lost her mom when she was two years of age. and has longed for her ever since. if you ever have a chance to see "high tide" with judy davis, directed by jane campion, do so. it's cj's favorite movie and it's a heartbreaker. so tender; that mother-daughter thing. we are so touched by our mothers. we are. i'm crying again, thinking of that movie, cj, rima, her mom, my mom. mama mia! this is too crazy. called my mother a few times this week; no answer. i hate that. she's either sleeping, can't hear the phone, or it's too far away from her. i miss my mom so much. a part of me is jealous that donna gets so much time with mom. my sister gets so short fused when i get there with so many questions about mom and what's up. we do talk a lot and e-mail; but damn, when i see mom, and spend time with her, i know there's a back story. it's different when you are always present or you come into the situation and have to catch up. mom seems to be getting very social. that is so good. she has "chosen" people to eat meals with. that's so unlike my mom. she seemed to have called a few "friends!" this is all good. now, if we can only keep her upright! i'm tired again, today. no energy. i think rima's mom and the cj mom scenario has just wiped me out. one "up" thing today; the new learning annex calendar is out and my super heroine marianne williamson is coming for an evening in the not too distant future. oh god, that's good. makes me feel so good. i wish she were my friend. i have qualities to offer her in a friendship. oh well. one day. regarding famous people: i have written some and they've responded! i started off as a kid with letters to tony curtis and janet leigh. as an adult there have been lily tomlin, katherine hepburn, liza minelli, shirley maclaine. good taste, if i say so myself! love human beings, famous or not, that are good souls. it's my appreciation of who they are and how they are that motivates me to contact them. it's really not so crazy. so goes today. thoughts. tears. worry. feelings. memories. life. it's life. love you, mom. love you so much.

May 27, 2002

it's all so complex and unforgiving. "it" being life. mom seems ok. ok in kingston, ok with eating. too many urine trips at night, stomach still aches, energy not too bad. i guess she's ok. christ, she's eighty-four. donna took her to dr. wenzke and we'll go to dr. ali when i get there. dr. wenzke wanted to see mom, now, just to check her meds. check her. he's so good. donna and ron have been dropping in a lot; they spend quality time with her on sundays. they had mom over after dr. wenzke's appointment too. so mom, indeed, is getting lots of attention. and yes, i'm jealous of that—that mom, donna and ron are there and i'm here . . . so far away. i'm busy; though not much work in the ol' film industry. caroline went to "the land" this weekend, that was good. a celebration of the jungian four-year course being half over. "the land" is a collective of old lesbian pals and friends from the "y" weekends of years past. nine original owners pitched in ten thousand each and bought an old farmhouse and sixty-five acres adjacent to crown land. over the years they've fixed it up; collectively run and peaceful. this is a model on how people and a property can get along. it's a wonderful place. i go up as often as i can. i actually tried to get some money to do a video on the land and the women; but couldn't get the money. after i went into so much debt developing a feature for eight years . . . and i truly believe i developed the cancer of my colon because of that intense stress . . . i'd never do anything like that again. not without the money upfront to cover all costs. it was a great idea, the "land video." intention is everything. on saturday, i picked up our frozen minced chicken and bought the dog veggies at the market. we make our own dog food; rather mix the minced chicken with mixed veggies we grind up. it's healthier for them. i cut, cuisinart, bag the veggies; takes a couple of hours. bought all the plants for the deck on saturday too. i was beat; did a lot. ended the day with a massage. very wise. my shoulders and neck are always sore; i carry my emotional baggage there. with the degenerative disk challenges in my back and neck, i'm always sore. aging sucks. went to my union meeting on sunday at 9:00 a.m. with sandra. i love driving. gee, i've been in transport for over ten years. did drive trucks but prefer vans as i get older. love driving cast and crew. love when i get those calls. sandra is also in transport. a fine soul. she knows the business well. she's very good at it. she's been my mentor, for years. i also had an emergency doggie "off leash" area meeting on the weekend. honestly life is just one thing after another. i can't stand life being too busy. i need my peace and quiet. too busy these last few days. now with mom in toledo, and so much traveling, and worrying, i'm a bit off. i don't handle intensity, at all. it does "feel" intense. maybe it's an astrological grouping. couldn't afford to get my astrology chart done the past few years. living close to the bone. i miss not having an idea of what's up. add caroline's hip and waiting for the hip replacement; seeing her limp and in pain . . . i'm drained. i hate seeing her so physically challenged. she doesn't complain. she keeps on going. i wish you all could meet her; she is such a fine human being. we've been waiting a year for hip replacement surgery. waiting on this one, popular, excellent surgeon. in ontario, there seems to be a lot of waiting for important things, medically. we've changed governments in the past and you wouldn't believe the cutbacks. it's insane. all this health challenge around me puts me in touch with my post cancer of the colon recovery. waiting for the five years, first day to happen. i do find stress challenging. i have no time for me. i hate that. i need that. i'm trying to develop my personal coaching business and there just is no time. you know starting a business, full- or part-time, takes a lot of effort. oh well. it'll all happen, eventually. then, as life would have it, this morning, our thirteen year old scottie, sammie, starts trembling. couldn't move her bowels on the beach. i freak. she seemed disoriented. i grab her and run off the vet. the last time i saw "that tremble" was when sydney, our schnauzer, had urine problems. we took him to emergency and in forty-eight hours we had to put him to sleep. cancer. oh god. the worst few days of our lives. we were devastated. the long and short of it—sammie was constipated! full of shit. thank god. why did this happen? don't know. there must be a lesson in all this; especially today. something to do with my attitude being full of shit? i think god is saying get a grip. shit happens. you have no control. let it go, girl. breathe. pray. give thanks. life. so much easier if you're in the now. i think of mom and i just want to sit by her side. sing "it's a wonderful world." wish she were here, in toronto, with us. generally, we really do live a peaceful life. lifestyle. but mom doesn't like dogs, real ones. i laugh when i think of her "cardboard" dog named lucky. she's had it for years. and a sign in her window, at home, beware of dog. oh, so many thoughts. the self pity is passing. just a busy time. thank you god, for being with me. for listening. i'm good. please bless my mom, god. be with her. help her ease into kingston. have some fun there. be healthy there! please, don't let her fall anymore. enough for now. i'll be with you shortly, mom. love you.

May 29, 2002

in mom's room at kingston; she's sound asleep. don't know how, with the loud noise from the air conditioning unit in the window. the central air is not on yet and mom needs it very cool for better breathing. like near cold. thank god they put in the window unit; i think it's helping. arrived yesterday. ride was ok; i find i get in touch with my anger and how upset i am regarding mom's condition on these rides. i can and do yell, scream, cry . . . pretty emotional, but a good outlet. i usually get angry with myself for being so out of balance; expect more from myself. i'm angry with caroline for being sick and going downhill; that damn hip. not her fault, of course, but you see how we humans transfer, how i transfer, all this shit. i don't think she's being aggressive enough with her doctor about the operation; but it's not "an emergency" and one waits. totally sucks. caroline is in pain; it hurts to watch her. i'm angry with mother for being on such a yo-yo journey. now, isn't that adult like! honestly, just overtired and can't handle all this. mom had been so kind, nice, generous, and somewhat loving since the bad pneumonia. she's not feeling well, again. she's being short, cranky, unpredictable. going into her "don't ask" syndrome. i hate that. it's so damn frustrating. i'm not good with it. yesterday i arrived around lunch; mom's still with her table. a somewhat warm welcome. then a resident (at the table) starts complaining about something and i suggest "take it to the resident's council."

mom curtly says, "don't get involved, it's not your business." that pushes my buttons and my reply is, smartly too, "it is my business, this conversation is my business, and if i want to suggest something, and mind you, it is only a suggestion, i will do that." that's how we started the visit. mom and i didn't have much going on after that. the woman, who had complained, and i, chatted. she was charming, interesting, and wanted me to guess her age. i went low. she surprised me with ninety-two! she was fabulous. so then, abruptly, lunch is over, mom's ready to return to her room. in the elevator mom states, meanly, "she's no more ninety-two than the man in the moon." i let it pass. no sense getting into it. oh yeah, mom, at lunch, yelled at one woman at the table, "don't touch my doughnut!" i was embarrassed. i excused myself to change a bit of clothing; went to the car. it was hot. met up with a woman from mom's table and she commented on how mom never says anything. she was happy to hear her protect her doughnut. i laughed hard. somehow mom managed energy to go out for pizza that night. one of her favorite outings. so off we go; mom, donna, ron, me. meeting nancy and elizabeth. it's such an easy statement . . . go out for pizza. it's like packing up a damn scout troop. pack the briefs, the walker, take mom in the wheelchair with all the attachments, her purse, sweater. it just seems to go on and on. donna and ron took mom; i followed. everyone was in a bad mood. just happens. life. minimal table talk. the pitchers of beer helped lighten us up, thank god. didn't take all the individual tension away, but helped. stuffing our mouths helped keep all our individual thoughts to ourselves. i stayed with mom a bit after the pizza; got her ready for bed and watched a bit of tv. i'm writing while watching tv; looking at her in bed occasionally. i don't like the sound of her breathing. she doesn't seem that well to me. not the best day. but, a day. we're all above ground. that's good. that's it for tonight, folks. later.

May 30, 2002

donna and i ran errands this morning. we never have enough sister time. i enjoy her. our "finest hour" was when she came to toronto, after my emergency cancer operation, and helped take care of me. we even had a few days up north, at the land. wonderful. i arrive in time for lunch and say to mom, "did you have a good night?" "don't ask!!!" i'm taken aback. "don't ask?" then mom demands, "get me up; i've got to go to the bathroom!" oh, i hate these kinds of moments. we get up, go to the bathroom and there's urine all over the floor and toilet. "mom, didn't you call for help?" "i did, but they didn't come in time." it's assisted living . . . the aides don't clean up the floor. housekeeping does. oh, i was so pissed. i was fuckin' livid. mom's saying "leave it!" i'm hysterical, "i can't leave it. it's filthy, it smells. it's not right." i'm repeating myself, "mother, did you call for help?" "don't ask!!!" well, i'm just friggin' gone. "mom, i deserve this information." "well, i'm not going to talk about it!" "well, i'll wait until you do!!!" "fine, i'll just sit here." well, i'm ballistic. losing it. dragon with full fire. bull wanting to charge . . . something, someone. it's during these moments i think i should take an anger management course. all caretakers should. this is indeed damn difficult. i call donna, tell her the whole thing, while mom's in her chair, "waiting." donna says "just leave it for now. check with all parties. we'll have mom in the car tomorrow . . . a captive audience and emphasize how important it is she tells us everything, as soon as possible." i wheel mom down to lunch. i am silent. mom knows i'm really angry. really angry. i suggest she eats with her friends; i'll eat alone. she won't have that. so we sit together at a table; with two others. i am not talking. fuck this whole place and the people in it. mature thoughts. mom asks me a few questions. i give as short answers as possible. i even say something like "what the fuck . . ." regarding something on the menu. a familiar waiter makes a face like . . . oops, stay clear of her. like he needs a healthy mature woman freaking on him. we come up after lunch; still the air is thick. mom goes right to bed. she's not feeling well; i'm so upset. i'm desperately holding onto the four agreements . . . don't take anything personally, do my very best, be impeccable with my words, don't assume. i'm asking for white light, pretend marianne williamson is in the room with me; sometimes that helps me with my behavior. sometimes i go right to having jesus with me. amma comes, too. at times, i just can't do this alone. i hate my mother when she's . . . what . . . so twisted. why can't she just bloody talk and give the story. i think, the pillow. the pillow over the head, as in bye-bye. who would know? i would. god. i couldn't; but honestly, i go there. haven't you? you will. at one point, you will. and then, guilt. the self disappointment that comes with that thinking. oui. we're human. we can be dark. a fact! i go snoop for the friggin' answers. did mom call? help get there? why can't someone just clean up the urine! i go to reception, the aides/nursing station. get the information. mom did ring for help, saying she was sick and vomiting. the licensed nurse practitioner on duty came up. asked if she should call family. mom said she had and didn't. she wasn't vomiting yet, just felt sick. nothing really done. but at least someone came. i don't know what happened regarding the pee and the mess. no call for bathroom help? mom has been going on her own, and sometimes it's a bit messy. we clean up the bathroom and toilet all the time. but more recently, mom's not making it. the rug is becoming messy. this time, it was more a mess than usual. she's just not calling for assistance, on a regular basis. i know that. it's assisted living. it's not nursing care. oh, mom is definitely in the gray area, here. this sucks. would you want your mom is a urine-saturated bathroom . . . floor, bottom of toilet, smelling? it's just not hygienic or right. this seems unacceptable. i don't know if mom is in the right place. donna, thank god and god bless her, drops in. but when i come, i stay throughout a day . . . a few days. i get to see a more in-depth, involved picture of the day to day. mom's strengths. her weaknesses. i could cry. i do. this is so sad. i think of every resident here; their challenges. their back stories. it is assisted living. i think mom's beyond assisted. she needs assistance. assistance living. mom's hair looks like shit. she'll get it cut and washed this saturday. we'll see dr. ali about mom's breathing tomorrow. this is so damn sad. i've cleaned up the bathroom. i hate the urine smell. it makes me gag. i feel like i'm going to vomit. i cry. i'm so sorry mother, so sorry you're not well. i can't imagine the humiliation you must feel, about peeing all over, messing beds, rugs, rooms. oh, this aging is very cruel. i've had it for today. i've had it.

June 3, 2002

home. toronto. on our deck. a sunny day. a good day so far: doggie walk, swim, some household chores. now, a bit of relaxation. living takes time, eh? i hated my visit. hated it. i don't think mom is that well. my sister has a higher opinion of mom's health. i'm feeling disappointed about many things. i can see that i'm worn out and down. thinking too much about others. not good. we took mom to see dr. ali, the pulmonary guy. her oxygen level is ok but she was ordered four breathing treatments a day. she should have had them since being released! the doctor who checked her out, an associate of dr. ali's, was negligent. honestly, this pisses me off so much. so much friggin' incompetence. and mom has both donna and i as witnesses. what happens to folks on their own? it's sad. sliding through the cracks . . . oh, so many. so, new medicine and treatments. most important, her room must be cool, cool, cool. mom likes it hot. here we go. we'll see how her thin skin and blood handle the cool. i'm drained. depleted. mom basically, just got here. oui. but i did go depleted to toledo. not good, at all. just too much going on for me. too many "things". not good with "too many things" anymore. it throws me. i can't handle it. i was just too busy before this last trip. things. for the home, for the dogs. life, really. then i went to toledo. i guess i just felt badly for donna working too hard; juggling so much. she needs more support! then mom and her challenges. her attitude and struggle. the drive. it was too much this time. i couldn't cope. i sank into a deep depression. the kind no one knows you're in. not very talkative. cried a lot. no one asked about me. funny how you can just be invisible. but, you are really there. life can have extremely problematic days for all of us, i think. more, maybe, than we care to acknowledge. saturday was mom's day over at donna and ron's. had a great rib dinner with nancy and elizabeth joining us. the neighbors dropped in. my grandniece and i played go-fish. donna and i took mom home, and i stayed a bit with mom. another breathing treatment and some tv. i couldn't wait to leave . . . for toronto. couldn't wait. sunday was renaissance unity and marianne williamson; fuel in my spiritual tank. thank god. thank god. i was out of gas. i filled up with super-high octane. anyone who doesn't know marianne, or ever experienced her and that church . . . it's remarkable. i kid you not. please check out either one of their web sites. her talk was on how much we need to pray, now! she's so down to earth, for an angel. she's just a doll. a light beam. so in my own metaphysical way, i left my sparrow wings in warren, and came home with my new eagle wings. my car was crowded but fine. i always get that visual of john travolta in "michael." what a great film that was. i realize i can act defeated about post-cancer, juggling mom and caroline and their health challenges, and my life. it's my attitude that needs changing, so i'm changing. who wants to be little when we are meant to be big??? who wants to be a little sparrow when you can be a friggin' eagle??? and so it is. repair. change of attitude. i find i can do those things when i have time, or take time. shut out the world. take the time. be with the silence. just worry about me. accept that everyone is on their own journey. let go and let god. be with god. pull myself up and out. be big. it's all an attitude. it takes time and energy to shape shift. i'm going to stop writing and pray. i'm going to be silent. i'm going to tend to my new big wings. god bless us all. renaissance unity. marianne. mom. donna and ron. caroline. our dogs. our cat.

everyone on the earth. god bless us all. may we all be big. big as we were all meant to be. big as we remember we can be. big. damn big. and so it is. amen.

June 5, 2002

my neck and lower back ache. i don't complain. i'd love to but there is too much going on with caroline and my mom. so i offer it up. why am i going to a rehab specialist? why not just rehab? who knows; i trust my doctor. i have an august 1st appointment. i had therapy with my fabulous dr. mary vachon yesterday. i am lucky to have dr. mary. we did a meditation, which was so sad. the guides that appeared in my meditation were marianne, amma, dr. mary, "heart," my make-believe pet elephant, and my dogs. well, in the meditation i went to a coal mine (family background . . . coal miners) and cried. cried. cried. the long and short of it was/is i have to understand my mom's childhood pain and sadness, which was/is very very deep. when she's not feeling well and is over-tired, that pain and sadness is very much a part of her unhappiness. she feels it. deeply. so i need to let her be . . . be in her pain . . . and pray for her process of it. consciously and/or unconsciously. i can't ignore that part of mom. simply can't. i can feel her pain and sadness; don't know it as intimately as she knows it, but i know it. we all know each other's pain. so says carl jung . . . oh god, i hope i have that right. collective unconscious. i got so much out of that session with mary. and marianne williamson, too; for in the meditation, i got a reminder from marianne. go to the mine and go in it, and get dirty. amazing, eh? mind-blowing, for those of us who relate to this kind of thing. as a reminder, i carry an imagined piece of coal with me. it made so much sense, to me. the whole experience. that's all that matters. may you . . . the reader . . . find what makes sense to you. i pray you try to understand your mom, dad, whomever. trying to understand takes work, can cause pain. but guess what, you'll come out a better person. oh sure, you may have to do some changing, some accepting, some eating of humble pie, some forgiving. get on with it. my god, how i've cried since that session. i've been thoroughly exhausted since. good, emotionally exhausted . . . when you know you understand something that's important. had a good sleep too, the night after. honestly, i encourage you to go on your journey. go. i love my mornings; the dogs and the cat are on the bed all wanting their morning loving. talking to. it's an exceptional moment. i love it. had a good day. doggie walk on the beach, swim, errands, and noon mass. it felt right. trying to remember to fit in the noon vigil for peace on the planet, as suggested by global renaissance alliance. that should be marketed by cnn . . . or a national paper . . . all papers. the good things in life, that will change things in life . . . why not support them? it's late in the day for me. i run out of energy late afternoon. just gone. i'm a sunrise to sunset person, a good jew because i think of "fiddler on the roof" and sunrise, sunset. i do feel jewish, by desire. i love each and every one of my jewish friends. i love their passion and compassion. energy. trying to be disciplined about starting my mornings with meditation and prayer. i find i'm so exhausted with this toledo, mom, worry thing. keep asking for the energy, my energy, to lighten up. feels heavy. too heavy. god bless you, mom. missing you so much today. thinking of your pain. so sorry mom. i'm carrying coal. god bless you. love you, mom.

June 7, 2002

i just love marianne williamson. she must be loved by so many. wonder if she feels it? god i want her to know about my eagle wings. how grateful i am. i read a quote from "the little prince" this morning, that made me think of her. "one sees clearly only with the heart. anything essential is invisible to the eyes." my heart seems aglow today. don't know why. it's a beautiful day. casey, the hound dog, is being so cute. balls and sticks . . . so in my face as i write this. this dog is an angel. a love. so is sammy. and barney. angels . . . all four-leggeds are angels. and mom . . . dear mom. angel. sometimes. hope it's this warm and sunny in toledo. that'll up her spirits. i can't imagine coming from sunny arizona to this dismal cold spring we've had . . . toledo is having. hardly a drop of sun. mom, although she's not a sun bunny, loves the bright sun and hot weather. in a lengthy conversation, donna reported that mom has been wearing the pads and underpants—not the depends— and wetting her pants and clothing a lot. mom didn't get her hair cut yet, which is also driving her nuts. i need to be in toledo more; donna can't handle all of mom's needs. mom needs more attending to. it's really affecting me, i feel so guilty being five hours away, but i need to work. i'm needed here for our home, the dogs, caroline's support. and damn, no call yet for her operation. this is so bad! i'm doing special exercises now out of "pain free" by pete egoscue. caroline has used this book forever, it seems. the exercises are preparing her for her operation. i just started with one set and it made my neck and shoulders feel so much better. i'll start to do them daily. time, living takes so much time. it takes all day to live. how do people work and live? it's impossible. thank god our mortgage is paid in august; then only the line of credit left. we need a financial miracle. it's coming. i can feel it. we're ok financially; i have little debt but no real resources. i've lived, traveled, taken risks. i'm month to month with very little for the future and old age, which i'm in. duh. scary. i'm not going to worry. i have a few years left in the ol' film industry and trying a few part-time, very probable, ventures. caroline has huge debts and fairly good future resources. we have a lovely bungalow in the beaches area; half a block from the water. we've steadily improved it and continue to do so. when mom dies i'll not get a lot of money. that's ok. but some. that's ok. when she dies . . . seems so strange to say that. she seems to have a resistance or her soul has work to do or it's just not her time. that is truly god's call . . . for each and every one of us, isn't it? i believe that. random death . . . like wrong place, right time . . . can't figure it out. i guess there is no wrong place. god created it all. and the path. and the plan. every so often i think we are an alien experiment. god could have created the aliens before us, and then they created us. it's a possibility, isn't it? whatever, the first and only source of energy . . . is the big kahuna. i think we'll all go back to the original fuse box. today, i feel love. i know i have love in my heart. these days are overwhelming. it's such a natural high, a natural feeling. must have meditated well today and emptied so i can just feel . . . what's to feel. mmm, this is good. i bless people at my metaphysical altar each morning. doing the noon prayer for peace in the world, as suggested by global renaissance alliance, co-founded by marianne williamson. oh god, i hope we don't self-destruct. i can only do what i can do; that's be loving. today, praying my ass off for mom, caroline, my family, and friends, and for peace in the world. it's a wonderful thing to be mindful and feel love in one's heart. it does change my actions. they seem softer. damn. today is about loving mom, loving people, peace on the planet. actually directing specific prayers toward that end. not everyday winds up like this. it's life. imagine if each of us did one thing, one thing today. that's a lot of "things" going out into the universe. i listened to a marianne williamson tape on transition last night. we are here as god's light and we are here to live with love for one another. duh. it isn't a difficult concept. oh god. be with us all today. i will channel love today. conscious effort. oh god, we're all so capable. help us know that. help us do something about it. and while i have your undivided attention god, especially bless my mom, today. thanks. and so it is.

June 10, 2002

preparing for another mother trip which means totally caring for me. dogs and beach time, prayer time, organizing time, some sun time. i hit the tennis ball with a neighbor today, for forty minutes. how great is that! so, thus far, taking good care of me and keeping that focus. i can sure handle free time. will handle retirement just fine. only a few years to go. if a lottery before, yippee! oh god, i'll be generous. i do love my work. i've always enjoyed working. it's all one thing; working, playing, living. but by god, one should enjoy his/her work. it's such a big part of us. bottom line: i just want peace and quiet. i love a home-operated business; i'm currently working on two. still "babies." part-time coaching practice; love birthing the practice. trained with the coaches training institute from san rafael, california. i've also created "sacred shopping," a personal introduction service. oh, i love and need time. time to work and play. to write my poetry, pray for peace, color . . . play with color . . . work on my comedy act, my one-woman show, my wedding. oh yes, i plan to marry myself, better put, celebrate the love for myself . . . after my five-year journey from cancer of the colon expires. yes, "marry" myself. an awesome radical act; a business opportunity. i can market this. this is a business! think about it; it's something each one of us could and should do. what's more important than loving one's self? then celebrating that love? think about it! drinking lots of water today, that's good. need to do that.

cutting down on alcohol. that's good. my emotional ride loves to take me to food and drink. not good. i've felt so down this last little while . . . the worry about mom gets me. i'm worrying when i'm not worrying. i can cry at the oddest times. something . . . a feeling, a word, something i notice . . . just on the street, can get me going. i love my mom so much. i just hate to see her in any pain, challenge. hate to see her losing it. it's hard to watch death, ever so slowly, come to the door. i guess that's what it is. when you're finally herded into assisted living, catered living, nursing homes . . . one seems to be waiting for death. that's it. it's not a great experience but one we will all go through, with a parent or parents. and what about us? where the hell are we going to be? i have no money to die with dignity. jesus. i don't. see, that's a worry. had an extraordinary weekend with caroline. we spend so little time together. we are partners, soul mates. our relationship works for us. i think the key is we're not sexual with each other and that just frees us. we are free. totally independent but partners. works for us. a lot of other lesbian couples, too. maybe it works in the straight world. it has to do with the ego. letting go. lots of work. but then, caroline is a psychotherapist studying to be a jungian analyst. and i'm . . . well . . . i've been in a lot of therapy, am on a spiritual journey that's pretty deep and committed, and i'm pretty damn smart. it's a beautiful and sunny day today. i love these days. this seems to be the spring of rain and cold; it's been very unpredictable. so sun, as bad as it is for you, i know, is so welcomed on this aging body of mine. i sunbathe nude on our deck, whenever i have a chance. we've got pretty good privacy. supposed to rain the next few days . . . so i'm not bothering to water the garden or the bushes. more time for me. yippee! checked in briefly with mom and donna yesterday; mom had a good day. her breathing is still labored. donna's adjusting medicine . . . again. mom doesn't sleep well. mom always has to pee. appetite goes up and down. water retention goes up and down. thank god, donna is/was a nurse and knows something about medicine and can suggest some things to the doctor. poor mom. takes too many friggin' pills, and god knows . . . they all have to work together. many times they don't. i think that drains me, too. some of the medicine makes mom cranky. there is always a positive and a negative to the damn pills. we either produce an alert but crabby old lady or we produce a sleepy person with no personality. it sucks. what a stupid drug culture we bought into. i have to actually prepare myself spiritually for the visits. i need to arm myself with all my "spiritual potions" . . . prayer, mantras, visions and "armor" whether it's light or a vibrational field around me. i get hurt easily with a remark or just no communication. i get hurt if anyone is "short." i don't know why i'm so ultrasensitive around my mom and this experience. i guess 'cause i love her so. and i'm like her. duh. so i get her. and yet, we have our journey. i wanted us to, i don't know, play cards, scrabble, sit, talk, talk, talk! have we ever done any of this? no!!! duh. how we want life to be and how it is. often, different. but damn, i'm holding a vision that it will be pleasant and loving. honest. my dear old friend stan, from chicago, is coming in to see mom. i'll be doing two different doctors with donna and mom. it'll be a busy time. i hope it's nice so she can at least sit outside a bit. maybe we can get ice cream. my mom loves ice cream. sunday, i'll do unity in warren. yippee! if mom wants to come over for dinner at donna's, i'll come back for that. i guess we'll be addressing the family reunion in southern illinois. donna wants mom to go. i don't think she should. it'll bloody wear her out. she gets down and it's so hard for her to come up. donna pushes mom; i'm more tender, i think. donna's intentions are good; see the family while you are living. a good thought. but, for me, a lot of buts. mom would get to see her sister, her brother, and lots of dad's family, and friends. that's mom's childhood area. i don't think she's up for it. the great thing, about the reunion date, is that i'll go to chicago first . . . to see my dear old friends nate and sue. they are truly like family. i miss them. she's in her mid-eighties . . . nate is early seventies. they are special. they love me, i love them, to bits. we met years ago; i had just returned from sierra leone, west africa. two years away. peace corps. they were teaching a peace corps group in chicago, going to . . . yes, sierra leone! i overheard their conversation in a restaurant and bingo . . . since that moment on, somewhere in '64, we became the best of friends. to know them is to love them. then there is amma. that's a story too, for yet another page. amma is in chicago for a few days in july; hugging the thousands who come to see her. god willing, i will be there, i will be hugged. after that chicago and toledo trip, it should be near caroline's operation, thank god. she is in so much pain, walks with a limp, a cane, and never complains. she is such an extraordinary soul. to know her is to love her. to bits. during all of this . . . in and out and traveling about . . . i'll work. oh please, i'll work. if i work two or three days a week, long hours, i make enough to get by. it's just right for my physical health, which i can never take for granted. for my mental health; which i can never take for granted. it's so easy to slip into "the glass is not so full," isn't it? generally, i'm good. the glass is usually very full. i'm blessed. i've always had a good attitude. i'm trusting my coaching will take off; and god knows . . . the sacred shopping is a good idea. now that i'm an eagle (marianne's talk rings in my ear) i'm flying high. i need inspiration . . . usually spiritual . . . then i can take off. that's why marianne, amma, my therapist dr. mary: are good for me. they inspire me. connect me to god. works for me. hope you have something that works for you. connects you with whatever you need connecting to. and don't be afraid of god. really. wonder what mom has as a connection? i think it was her church in sun city. working with st. vincent de paul. the people. good people. i trust mom prays . . . but i don't know. she's hard to get into those conversations. she does get communion once a week. she doesn't read anything anymore. clips coupons for donna, now and then. my spiritual needs are met by a good service. i wish i could get my mom, donna and ron to go to renaissance unity in warren. when i can't get to toledo and warren, i sometimes attend religious science centre of toronto. it's pretty cool. i attend my universal fellowship metropolitan community church of toronto with rev. brent hawkes, often. now that's an awesome church and service. and brent. fantastic. i love church, but then, i love god. i love to experience god in community. i feel so blessed to have an open and receptive heart regarding god. i was raised a catholic. mom was pretty devout. i am "collapsed" with the catholic stuff. it's too dark. not inclusive enough. not positive enough. i'm getting tired of writing. sometimes i feel drained; exposing my heart. my thoughts. but this is what it is, now. exposure. about so many things. my god, this is challenging. thank you god. thank you god for guiding me to doing this. i just would not have remembered all of this. mom's journey. all the thoughts connected with it. thank you god. and god, bless my mom today. i hope she's praying. i do. i always found it so helpful. find it so helpful. be with mom. please. be with her. god bless you mom. hope you have a good day. see you very soon. love you, mom.

June 13, 2002

here in mom's room, it's very cool. and cool outside. mom's doing remarkably well with it all. i know it's not easy for her. but if she doesn't have it cool, it'll be game over with the breathing. yesterday, i left at 5:17 a.m. for some reason i noticed the time exactly. i got here by 10 a.m., in time to catch donna and ron. we all went to mom's. she is having some big test for her stomach. ron took my car. i stayed with donna and mom. it wasn't a bad experience, for mom. the test was negative, which was good. dr. padda said her stomach looked fine; small hiatal hernia, but nothing to be concerned about. he'll do an ultrasound of mom's pancreas and liver. she's been vomiting again, so we're checking out what possible causes there are. mom's a roller coaster, some days bad with all kinds of stuff, some days, good functions. every day a new adventure. today, she's low energy, tired, not in the greatest of moods. when we went to dr. wenzke today, mom had gained ten pounds in two weeks! water? food? what? we're a bit alarmed. she's retaining something. he's upped the lasix to two a day and wants her to elevate her feet higher than her heart as often as possible. he'll see her in a week to ten days. mom does have congestive heart disease and emphysema; not a good combo. her water retention seems to be on the rise. we've taken her off zoloft; she's not as sleepy but will most likely be crabby. with the increased lasix, she may be up during the night. honestly, one thing is good for some things, bad for others. the medicine juggle is something else. so many are not compatible but all are necessary. so who loses? the person downing them. i find the whole medicine thing sad. i've come more prepared this time. i was so drained the last trip. everything got to me. i prepared myself much better spiritually; very close connection with god. staying close, too. i feel sorry for my sister . . . not one fun thing as a release . . . or at least that i can see. i must talk to her about this. we're so different on how we live and manage our lives. she could get a massage once a week, that would be so good for her. donna looks so stressed to me. stan, my very dear old friend from chicago, came to visit mom yesterday. he took the train, stayed at the ramada inn suites, downtown toledo. i finally got him in between doctor's appointments. we had a family gathering at jo-jo's, a popular pizza parlor near donna's. then we brought stan back to mom's place. stan and i watched tv with mom. it really was nice of him to come; he's been part of the family for years. i took stan back to his inn; he left this morning. well, it's time to wake up mom for dinner. to be continued. god bless my mom. we all love her dearly.

June 17, 2002

time does fly. be aware. the most important aspect about living is, are your moments all they can be? that's my take on it. i'm home, about to go for a tennis hit, with a neighbor. my favorite thing, tennis. just hitting. so . . . zen? it makes me feel so alive! thank god for marianne and renaissance unity. they keep me going. fill my spiritual tank. kept me going this past visit. helps me with mother's journey. as does my therapist, dr. mary vachon. wow. what a woman and therapist. it takes a village to help my life! god bless our villages, therapists, partners, friends, family, pets, causes, passions, our god! so many balls to juggle. god isn't really one of the balls. he's much more. but you get the picture. it takes a village just to live! called mom last night upon arrival, after six, thinking she'd be at my sister's. but no, she didn't want to come over for sunday dinner. man, i hate that. that was one of the primary reasons for bringing her to toledo. "mom, you'll never have a sunday alone, anymore!" duh. what we hope, plan, and vision doesn't necessarily happen. she wanted to be left alone. it was a busy week. doctors on wed.,thurs., friday. company wed. lunch and a hair cut out of the building, thurs. then i was there for lunch, before her doctors appointment on friday. so it was busy. too busy. just one of those things. i know on friday night, her regular bath night, they didn't come till 10:30 p.m.! they had an emergency. well, mom was so pissed off. on saturday, she was left too long at the dining room table, after breakfast, to be wheeled back to her room. she was pissed off, again. i guess she flipped out. angry. i'm proud of her for that. the kingston people did apologize. things happen. they just do. they made a "new pact" be more on top of mom. mom was satisfied. i stayed for lunch saturday. spent the afternoon. mom is beginning to hate when i stay for dinner. it's $12. i don't mind, but she hates when either she or i pay $12. thinks it's too high. it's $5 for lunch. that's ok. lunch is a pretty darn good meal. so i left her once i wheeled her to dinner saturday. she seemed to want her independence. i hope i got her signals right. it afforded me the best visit with my sister. i got to donna and ron's; donna and i got to sit in the backyard, have a cocktail and yak. it was fabulous. her backyard is gorgeous. mom was supposed to get bathed saturday night. maybe she was just exhausted sunday. she didn't sound good, when i finally caught up with her at kingston. i'm half expecting an emergency call, don't know why. i feel mom wasn't all that well. my intuition. god only knows if i'll make the roycht family reunion july 5 and 6 in southern illinois. all the cousins are supposed to meet at uncle tony's place; across the road from cousin bernie's. we did this two years ago at cousin billie and tom's, in barrington, illinois. that was a good scene. the roychts are a bit more together than the kerins. i guess it's the croatian blood that makes the kerins a bit more . . . well, not so dysfunctional as emotional and hotheaded. it's in our veins. the roychts are physically located closer together; the kerins scattered to the winds. east to west. i know mom would love to see her brother johnny, who isn't all that well. her sister, barb. god bless her. she's so kind to all of us. the whole family. god willing, mom will be able to make the trip. donna and ron want to go; take mom. i'd go in my car; donna and ron, mom, nancy and elizabeth, and scruffy, in donna's big van. and all of mom's shit; the breathing machine, etc. a lot. damn. my tennis hit just got cancelled. damn. the weather is not cooperating! i'm off on a walk! i'm really putting an effort into mind, body, heart, soul. mindfulness. in all areas. it works. so god bless my mom today. i love her so. hoping she's having a good day! god bless marianne and the church today. i do get filled up when i attend. it's awesome. i get so spiritually centered, focused, goal-oriented. god bless them all. staff, and supportive people. being in transport, in the movie industry, i can't tell you how much i appreciate it when a star who's won at an awards ceremony, thanks the crew. it's the same in all walks of life. the "star," the "church," has a staff who makes it work! marianne. she walks her talk. i'm remembering sunday, after service, i observed her talking to any and all who lined up to chat with her. she listened. she looked at them. cared. was real. that's good, folks. that's good. she's good. authentic. human. and she's darn smart. must have a photogenic memory. she quotes this person, that person. remembers many facts, figures. god bless you, marianne. i'm at the age where i'm starting to forget. it's a bitch! i wish my mom could experience marianne. would she get her? i think she would. mom would have to meet her. then she'd think, "oh, what a nice lady." oh mom, hope today is a good day for you. i'm off on a walk. to be in the moment. to pray. to think. to feel. follow my mindful path. thank you god. i guess this is what is supposed to happen. thank you. take care of mom today. please. guide me. use me. and god, bless all of us and our villages. we're all so interconnected. all so important to and for one another. let us not forget that. thank you, god. come walk with me on the beach. time together. this is good. love you, mom.

June 26, 2002

8:32 a.m. sitting in a cube truck; on set for the camera department on a show called "oydessy 5." parked at the corner of davenport and hallum avenue, in toronto. raining. i love this. i love transport. today i'll pretty well be in the cube truck, left alone. quiet. i have a visual on the camera guys. i'm protecting the truck. we'll move locations partway through the day. only one move. at that point, we'll be near the production office and crew parking. it'll be a long day. but easy. i love this, as i get to pray my little heart out, journal, think, do walking meditation around the truck. read the papers. catch up with the news. we're shooting almost seven pages; i won't have much to do. when the show wraps, camera will load the truck, i'll drive it to the parking lot. probably a sixteen hour day. never have been on this show so i don't know their speed. i'm tired. had good friends laurie and dom for dinner last night. extremely busy folks; filmmakers. dinner on the deck. they waited for caroline to get home after her group, to say hi. i didn't get into bed till after 11 p.m. up at 4:30 a.m. i don't think i'll work tomorrow, need a good sleep. will do ok for money with one day's work. need to be as healthy and centered, balanced and rested as i can be for this next trip; lots of driving. leave for toledo this coming friday. go to southern illinois the following thursday. chicago in between. very busy. excited to see mom. nephew nick in from phoenix. that'll be fun. can't wait for chicago. for nate and sue. for amma—who is doing her north american tour. need those hugs from amma. southern illinois should be fun. two family reunions really. the roycht reunion but so many kerin relatives in the area. it all happens starting july 4th. i love my family. both sides. mom and dad used to send donna and i, when little, to southern illinois each summer. we had a blast with our cousins, aunts and uncles. we were very close to our first cousins on dad's side; bette and billie (wilma). my god, we had fun. i think donna has had her challenges with mom these past two weeks. mom has had a spell of diarrhea, again. not wearing her depends; instead pants and pads. her clothes, the bathroom floor, the rug in her apartment all have been a mess. and stinky. she should be in something else. diaper? who knows. mom's breathing has sounded bad to me. i think she should be on the catered side of kingston—she's too much in the grey area. she needs more care! the assisted side is for those who can really take care of themselves. mom is too questionable. she does have an alarm wrist band on but never pushes it! i guess it's a pride issue. if she pushes it, she claims she has to wait and "they" come too late. when i don't see her for several days, she always seems to go down a rung on the ladder. so, we'll see; i think we're to have saturday night together. that'll be good. if i'm needed while in chicago, i'll race right back. whatever. this is a big trip, big deal. god willing, it'll all go well. god, please be with mom for this. it's important.

July 8, 2002

afternoon. it's a blur but i have highlights. i spent the best night ever with mom, july 4th. i had gone to her hospital room to watch july 4th celebrations on tv. as a yank; i'm a dual citizen, i'm so proud of american celebrations. no one does it better. we're so big. there was such a choice: new york, washington, boston. you can't beat that washington background; our heritage, our symbols. those national monuments have so much meaning. the music, the choreographed fireworks; it goes on and on. an everlasting orgasm. let's back up, though. i have to catch up myself. i left for toledo-chicago-the family reunion-on friday, june 28. nick was in toledo. it was to be a great time. i love nick; we have a blast together, very comfortable with one another. mother wasn't that good on friday. or saturday. she complained of a new pain, in her hip and leg. around the area where the hip replacement was done this past february. so she was taking pain killers that made her pretty sleepy. she was uncomfortable for the most part. it didn't feel right. mom looked bad. i had lunch with her on sunday; she cried at the table and was miserable. i wheeled her to the room and called donna and ron, wondering if we should take her to emergency. mom didn't want to go; donna and ron were taking mom to dr. wenzke monday afternoon anyway; an appointment that had been set. donna suggested pain pills; mom was ok with that and fell asleep. i went back to donna's; we talked and both felt i could hit the road to chicago. they didn't need my help monday. donna would keep a close eye on mom. so i drove to chicago; it had been a year since i had seen my very dear friends sue and nate. i wanted to see them desperately. i arrived around 6, chicago time. i had no trouble with my favorite route into the city; off the skyway onto the lakeshore. nothing, nothing, nothing like our chicago lakeshore. every city should have been designed like this . . . if they had a lake, that is. a busy day in chicago with the taste of chicago and gay pride day. i lived on the near northside upon return from africa; old towne. a blast. the 60's. just a blast! so much fun, so much energy. what a time. i'm sorry for anyone who didn't get a hit of the 60's. we had a fabulous sunday night at nate and sue's. joanne, their best friend, joanne's straight daughter who had participated in gay pride day . . . and a few others. yakking, eating, laughing. so great. chicago is one of my true homes. i love the city (near north and northside, the lake) if i ever could afford it, i'd have an apartment there. a writing place. i feel so creative and alive when in chicago. maybe one day. monday was tethered to nate and sue all day. we were a trio. just hanging. so delightful and comfortable. we just have fun, doing nothing. how good is that? then my good friend pat came over with videos. we ate leftovers and watched videos. so enjoyable. i think god sent a joint to share, too. that was fun. i do that rarely. so rarely. once every few years. just don't need to. i'm high on life and living. here's what i know about grass: the worst grass in the world is far too strong for me. that tells you how i can handle it. i do like being natural. pure. aware. i'm a drinker. i drank in the 60's while everyone smoked. my sister called. damn. mom was put in the hospital right after seeing dr. wenzke! he felt there was something wrong, but didn't know what. damn. he was going to try to get to the root of the pain. i decided to go ahead with monday's plan to see amma; sue, pat and i were to go. then i'd head back to toledo. so one whole morning and afternoon with amma. sue and i got our hugs; sue loved the experience. seeing amma, the whole experience of love, smells of india, feeling of peace. it's just remarkable. amma is truly someone sent by god. i returned wednesday a.m. and went straight to the hospital. mom seemed weak to me, but ok. they had done many tests as well as dr. wenzke sending in an orthopedic man to assess the leg and hip pain. bad weekend to try to get test results; holiday weekend. many folks have it off; and rightly so. i had a nice visit with donna and ron; spent a lot of time at the hospital with mom. so that brings us up to july 4th. what was so special? for some reason mom felt like talking and i was a good listener. a good combination. doesn't happen often. we talked honestly about the future; her desire to be in arizona with hired help. she didn't want donna and ron in the house, with the dogs. she can't stand the barking. drives her nuts. she is used to quiet. well, hell, she lives alone with a cardboard dog. she feels donna and ron are too busy. they are always busy. mom likes peace and quiet. i can see mom's side. donna and ron are alive, well and enjoy their life style. life is busy. mom needs it quiet and calm, she's limited physically, and doesn't feel well. oh mom. mom can go off people. she's done that with all of us. i think now, she's really off the dog(s). it's mom's journey. in my heart, i know that it's caused by pain. pain that she can't share. pain that she probably can't describe. shared some of this conversation with donna. it didn't sit too well. i feel mom has chosen her home, as to go home, over her daughters. that's painful but i can understand it. i know what home means to me. can't imagine not being home, having a home. so i don't know what'll happen. will mom go home? when? hire help? donna and ron, and dog(s), go? stay where? i mean, who knows. they have to talk. i've encouraged mom to talk honestly with donna and ron. to share. i've encouraged donna to have the donna, ron, mom talk but set it up so everyone can be honest, cry, and speak from the heart. so i don't know if they'll do that. mom was transferred to lake park on friday. it bloody well takes all day.

still in pain. i don't think we have any real answers. we went saturday to have lunch with mom. she was having an anxiety attack; not able to breathe. they gave her some major mother of a pill; zonked her out for a day or so. she calmed down and saw the respiratory aides, nurses. finally, everything starting to go a bit better, be a bit lighter. we had stopped in saturday night; she was ok. resting. lake park is really fine; it just seems bit small and crowded. little rooms. mom is in a double. she's not eating yet. that's not good. i went over sunday a.m. if she had not been well, i would have stayed. she seemed ok. so i followed my plan to drive to warren, and then home. needed a dose of that renaissance unity. donna and ron were going to drop by after church. i prayed all the way to warren. marianne was not going to be there but rev. jim lee was. i like him. he's not marianne, but i needed that church, the music, the people. i needed god . . . in that setting. it was an excellent service. then home. as i said, i love my home. caroline. casey. sammie. barney. all my stuff. my routine. everything in the house. called when i got home; donna and ron weren't home, i called mom. she sounded so much better. i cried. mom said, "i feel so much better after the operation." oops. mom . . . duh, no operation. maybe it was the medicine talking. we talked a little. i cried after the phone call. then donna called to say the ortho man showed up while they were there for lunch. he was called because of mom's constant pain. he gave mom some cortisone injections. donna "assisted." so mom did have "an operation!" thank god. mom knew what she was talking about. another cry. a happier cry. mom feels so much better. well, that's the story. till now. amazing. mom, what a journey you're on. god bless you. i truly hope god is blessing you. love you, mom. later.

July 27, 2002

i noticed my last entry was july 8th. i just don't know how i can let things go this long without recording. i'll do my best with "things," as "things" happen so fast. they do. that's life. mom is still in lake park and loving it, as i see it. she's had a good stay. loves it there; the nurses, the nurses aides, the physical therapists. she's had, this time, another two great roommates. carlene, her present roommate, is just lovely. they all have been. mom, after the cortisone shot, has been so good. she's gotten much stronger in physical therapy again. her attitude and spirits are high. she's had infrequent respiratory/anxiety attacks. that is so great. she'll be moving back to kingston this coming week. my last trip was one of the best. i usually arrive expecting the worst . . . and she looked so good to me. that was july 17th, around noon. or the 18th. i'm so lost. i pretty well spent the day and evening with mom. did so till i left on friday, july 19th, around two, for the peace conference at renaissance unity in warren, michigan. that's fodder for another book! a good book! a necessary book! my god, i hope we all wake up to our potential. about each and every one of us being responsible for peace. if each one of us just woke up to our own potential. our own connection with the higher being, call it what you may. and live that. what a world. i was kind of anxiety ridden myself, to leave, as donna and ron were going to go "quickly" to germany. one can do that, being retired army. they drove to delaware, caught an army transport, and presto . . . germany. to see the family and kids. it was an important quickie; as sharon had had a thyroid challenge, was to get an iodine treatment for four days, be in the hospital. so presto, donna and ron appear. they miss those grandkids so much. and why not? they're the best, as all grandkids are. donna and ron left sunday morning. i called donna on saturday night from the conference; all was well. they did leave; nancy and elizabeth saw mom on sunday, i believe, and i showed up, after the conference, at around 7:30 p.m. stayed with mom till around 9 p.m. we were on the same page; so it was so good. every time mom bounces back, for me, it seems we connect in a better way. a more loving way. i was so happy to be there; and then go home to scruffy and penny, the dogs; be with them. being a dog lover, i know an owner, as well as the dog(s), need the contact. monday our highlight was going to the cafeteria, with mom in her wheelchair. after therapy. i had to get some breakfast. physical therapy had given mom coffee. she just wanted to be with me, while i ate something. we had a nice day and evening. tuesday, they took mom off oxygen, for a bit, and with the freedom, i suggested we go outside. it was a non-humid, lovely day. not too hot. sun shining. mom wanted to be in the sun. my god, how nice that was to see her, have her outside. i looked at mom in her chair, in the sun, hearing the birds, the blue sky with lovely fluffy clouds. it was a wonderful moment. rare. truly wonderful. i've just been so relaxed within myself, with the help of marianne williamson's sermons at renaissance unity, her tapes, and her books. i feel she's helped me lift myself up. really become an eagle, no more sparrow. it's helped so much with mom. i am myself. i talk with no holds barred. i stand up for myself. i listen to mom, and she listens, and when she's had enough, she lets me know. and we, somehow, move on, in an easier fashion. we have immediate closure when i'm too much for mom, in a pleasant way. i have no agenda. i have no cross to bear. i have forgiven. i am at peace with mother. do you know what that's like??? it's been about a forty-year journey for me. proof . . . that time is an illusion, focus is important, and healing is possible. but i had/have faith. i do believe in a higher power. is it an actual being? i don't think we'll ever know till we "get there." but certainly, there is something so powerful, mighty, beyond any imagination, that created the whole damn thing. including us. the whole damn thing. and that's what i believe. a course in miracles, marianne williamson, metaphysics, make it easy for me to grow in that belief. live a much easier life, right here, right now. my, my. is that pleasant. especially for me . . . a former type a. driven. so driven i couldn't, in reality, stand myself! ahh. it's good. life is good right now. even with mom, flirting with passing. now it's a flirtation. it's interesting. i left for home wednesday morning, after stopping by mom's for a coffee. she was good. i miss her, when i leave her. when we talk, she shares that she loves me and misses me. i do the same. it's simple, honest, clean. i called yesterday; she was helping carlene with filling out the food menu for the next day. mom's even getting generous and nice, with all people. that's lovely. if you could witness her personality in physical therapy; mother teases, jokes, shares. she blossoms. it's such a shame we can't keep them, the aging folks with challenges, in those situations where they get the exercise, the attention, the stimulation, the right food, the doctors checking up, and the nurses' compassion . . . at some constant level. i fear for mom returning to kingston and the assisted living situation. although "they" look in on her, it's just not the same. the next step would be "catered" or a nursing home/level of care. i think it would depress mom to be in that situation. but she actually needs that level of care. i did go to luthern village, in toledo, as we are looking, in case there's one more level in between. and by god, that was wonderful. so damn expensive. out of reach, really. and so it is. many thoughts, feelings. all i know is, i love my mom, so much today. so much.

August 6, 2002

there's quite a break in between entries; just too much to juggle in my life . . . the dogs, cat, caroline, financial responsibilities, challenges about working, and keeping on spiritual track. hard. that's what we do in and with life, we juggle. some days all the balls fall, some days only one or two. it's hard to stay on top of "both" my lives; one in toronto, one in toledo. here i sit in room 222, kingston residences, watching tv. today, it's about planning the remembrance of 9/11. that's another "thing" isn't it? as an american it's such an ongoing sorrow. it is. i'm still sad. what a remembrance it will be . . . 8:46 a.m. silence to begin; first plane. 10:29 a. m. second plane. then time for pennsylvania. the pentagon. oh my. the heart weeps. we, i mourn each person. i pray for all those gone, those that remain; families left behind. those who caused the evil. what is their afterlife journey like? i'm curious about that. can we reach the tortured souls, with evil instilled, before any more evil acts? doesn't matter who they are; can we reach them? who can reach them? what will make them change their attitudes, actions? that is the biggest question of all, isn't it? what good, really, does it do to pray for them? will they feel it? another culture, another god, another leader, no concept of freedom, compassion, love? will my prayers reach them? gotta talk to marianne about this. enough on that. put my own nose in a course in miracles, again. i'm here with dear mom. snoring. i know i snore. inherited? or an individual thing? it's damn cold in here. the physical therapist coming at 1:30. i'm about to get mom up for lunch. it's going to be a day! donna will come over after work (around 4) and we'll talk about mom getting back to lake park. the upper floor, nursing. extended care. whatever they call it. my god, my god. i didn't think we'd be doing this . . . talking about mom in hospitals and extended care. i just thought she'd come and be here. we'd have fun. well, if not fun, it would be nice. this sucks! mom needs care. bottom line. yesterday mom and i talked and cried. mom feels she is going downhill, wouldn't make it, would feel safer in a hospital, doesn't think she'll see "home." she feels so sad about that. maybe christmas. maybe she'll make it back for christmas. maybe not. she cried. she'd love to go home. i would love for her to go, too. i didn't know what to say. in those moments, it's just sad. it was honest. but so sad. mom just hasn't been right for any extended time since being here. don't know why. mom does like the attention in extended care. why not? meals in your room; eat bedside. people come to take you to therapy. you have a roommate. and they change. nurses change with their shifts. therapists change with shifts and days off. there is variety, movement, life. why wouldn't that be preferable to loneliness and isolation even if self-imposed? kingston is wonderful, really. mom is beyond assisted living though. and she's just not social. of course the staff does its best to get residents out of their rooms. but the older, less social ones? they don't change. loners. not good. mom got up, reluctantly. she actually slept on and off through lunch. i reminded her of a therapy session after lunch. she didn't want to do it. started whining and crying "can't do it." of course i said, "you've got to try, mom." she gave me the look. oh god. but she did it!!! no enthusiasm or joy, mind you. but she did it . . . at times with her eyes shut. i shook my head. oh, this is not good. oh, this is not good.

August 7, 2002

when i came in today, mom was sleeping in her chair. when she woke up, she shared that she had fallen around 5:30 or 6:00 a.m., in the bathroom. i couldn't believe it. i immediately asked if she was in pain, if we should go to the hospital. she said she was ok; bruised, cut, but ok. fell on her right side. she was leaning over to pick up her briefs, a pad, her depends. one of those. she tried because we keep harping on her "try to keep moving, try to be independent, mom." well, has that come to haunt us or what! i then went on my lecture of "when someone is with you mom . . . be brave . . . but when alone, call for the f.... help!" try for us, for the physical therapy lady . . . but when alone, get help for whatever. i was so sorry for mom. her right side is her vulnerable side; having had several operations on her right shoulder, her right hip replaced. and i think she gets the cortisone shots on her right side. at any rate . . . right is not good. well, the day has progressed. it's 3:10 p.m. mom's taking a nap. we just had a fire drill but i don't think it was planned. everyone was quite confused, including mom and me. we got as far as the opposite side of the hall. then an all-clear. thank god. we had lunch on the patio today; they had a hot dog cookout with dogs, chips, potato salad and lemonade. we, then, actually sat in the sun. i believe it was the first time mom has been out in days. the weather hasn't been the best. too humid for her. her condition. when the sun is out, mom loves sitting in it. she misses the warmth of arizona. badly. she's in that damn cool, cold room all the time. the sun is a very welcomed friend. that damn emphysema. really, since we brought her here, she's been through hell. i don't know if we're back. pneumonia, two different hospitals, same extended care facility a few times. she's been very weak. i think she's lonely, unhappy, anxious. has had some pretty severe anxiety attacks. i think too, she perceives her relationship with her grandson as being severed. he doesn't call as much. he may try, but she doesn't hear the phone. sometimes she's not near it. the phone thing isn't working well, at all, for her. she feels the physical separation. she really misses nick. i don't think he was overly attentive when here, either. i think that broke mom's heart a bit. he can't take the old age picture. it's pretty brutal. hard to get used to, if one does. mom's not the easiest. but . . . she's the displaced person here. i do feel badly for mom. it's a rotten road she's on. i don't think mom should be here, after the fall. i just don't. here, as in kingston. she'll be bloody crippled! one more fall . . . too big a risk. we've got to do something different. i'll go home tomorrow morning and worry till i get back. she looks bruised and banged up. her cough, well, it's no great shakes. i'm really worried. it's an intense time. caroline's operation coming up; getting her hip replaced, finally. we've waited so long. sammie's skin condition not good, an allergy thing. financial stress. damn. oh well . . . so easy to go there and feel . . . i don't know, like it's unfair. who gives a flying ——? it's my only mom, who bloody well sacrificed for me. my sister. so much. damn. i love my mom. this trip donna and ron seemed stressed too. perhaps the stress of the upcoming military reunion? they are a committee of two! that's not enough, really. i've tried to help a little, here and there, with some things on the computer. i am concerned about donna. she doesn't relax enough. pretty hyper. doesn't exercise at all. a bit of walking. gives so much of herself away. i'm just realizing i worry a lot about donna. jesus. i'm overtired. maybe that's all this is. being overtired. worried about mom. donna. caroline. sammy. the world. this damn diary. my neck is so sore. i hate that. i'm stretching and exercising each day, make sure i walk. not eating right. drink a bit too much. stressed out. oh, i need marianne and renaissance unity this sunday. every sunday! i so need that experience. i do have a good spiritual practice. my best friend is god. that's good. feels good. feels right. hello god, help me. i'm a bit lost in thought today. well, donna should be here shortly. oh mom, i sure hope you feel loved, pampered, taken care of, concerned about. you must feel happy with us; especially donna. hell, she's here daily. it may be a quick visit, on the days when there's not an outing, but mom . . . you are so cared for. we love you so much. hope you are feeling it as deeply, warmly and freely as it's being offered, given. thank you, god, for the time. for the opportunity with mom. and with family. be here with mom, please, be here. please keep her upright! please, god.

August 13, 2002

for some reason, i'm into an inspirational message from "a return to love," by marianne williamson. one of the great books of our time. don't know why it leaped out at me, but it did. i guess i needed it today. it says, "in god's world, the more we give, the more we have. we needn't compete, in business or anywhere else. our generosity towards others is key to our positive experience of the world, in the world. there's enough room for everyone to be beautiful, to be successful, to be rich. it is only our thinking that blocks the possibility from happening." and the prayer attached to it was, "there is enough of everything, for everyone. i open my heart and love flows through me." wow. isn't that just one fantastic wow! enough said, enough to think about today.

August 19, 2002

i think i got as far as the date yesterday. it's really august 20th. watching a lifetime movie made for tv. mom's room. 3:35 p.m. will write till donna arrives. so much has happened. mother made another miraculous recovery! yet again! she really has. it's been so great. this past week, she told donna or rather asked donna, if she could stay, at least until christmas, maybe permanently! donna called and was so happy. mom had wondered if it was ok with ron. donna said yes, yes, yes!!!! amazing. amazing. god bless mom. god bless the process. god bless you, god. it's a miracle. and what is a miracle? . . . a shift in thinking. a shift. they happen all the time. we just don't stop and see them, feel them, acknowledge them. thank you, god. god bless you, mom. i'm overwhelmed. thank you, god, again. i think i shared that when mom rallies, she goes into a nice phase. maybe she felt, "hey, this isn't so bad." who knows? or may-be she's feeling this is safer, why fight this? i don't know. i don't care. all i can tell you is i'm so happy. mom's here. close by. i get to visit. yahoo. thank you god. thanks for talking to my mom. oh please, though, keep her upright. healthy? can i ask for her health . . . to be good? oh god, thanks. just simply, thanks.

September 9, 2002

been too long since last entry. too long. mom's good. that's the good news. she's been on an up. i think it's because she's made the decision to stay. through the holidays? longer? i think she's really thinking. god bless her. she really was so upset about going back with donna and ron and the dogs, penny and scruff. it was driving her nuts. the alternative? a stranger in her home? twelve-hour shifts; two strangers? nah. wouldn't be good. mom would hate someone in her kitchen, moving her stuff, using her stuff. whoa nellie. it wouldn't fly. so, maybe she's thinking, this ain't so bad. i've the kids, family. great support. a nice place. mmmm. i do feel she's settling into kingston. her dining pals. a routine. and she loves all the caretakers. it is challenging. she's in "gray." no doubt about it. that's my perspective. she's alone too much. she's tired a lot. sleeps, watches tv. she's ok with that. that's what she's been doing the last few years. i think a big change came after her car accident, in arizona, a while back. mom was lucky not to be killed when a mack truck hit her. after that, there was a decline in her driving. she drove just a bit. come to think of it, that may have truly started this last, big, downhill slide. she does get out a fair amount here. well, donna, ron, and mom went off to a family wedding in southern illinois this labor day weekend. donna said it was quite the challenge and tiring, but mom was remarkable, really. a few very challenging moments but overall, it went well. god bless my sister. she's a driven woman. god bless her. i've been home. caroline's hip replacement was on august 29th. it went well. she feels good. started moving right off the table. she's unbelievable. it feels good to be in one spot. especially when that spot is home. thank god that damn operation is over and all is well. feels good to have mom feel so good; she had a fabulous time on the trip. loved the wedding. loved seeing everyone. amazing. an amazing phase we are in. thank you, god. i'll go back to toledo when the military reunion is on; donna and ron will be at a downtown toledo hotel. i'll stay in the house, take care of the dogs, see mom. a good plan. i'll get to go to church too, in warren. damn if marianne isn't leaving the church, come january 1. i'm so sad. but, i guess, the long and short of it is she's a writer, lecturer, and the church has its own agenda. i'm not so sure they can handle an angel in the place. amazing, eh? i'll see as much of her as i can; i'm already having separation anxiety. my spiritual food. i'll get too thin! i'm now a good caretaker for my darling caroline. she's just motoring along with her physical therapy. her recovery. so, so much to be grateful for. so much. and i am. truly, i am blessed. today, i feel so very blessed. i hope you are blessed, as well. we all deserve the very best. and that best comes with an attitude. check yours. i'm checking mine right now and damn, it's good. thank you god. god bless mom. later.

September 27, 2002

late afternoon. a running commentary on mom, for donna and ron; they are hosting ron's military reunion. mom's dry coughing today; has been in bed all day. we did eat but she says she can't keep her head up. she had bad pee pants this morning! did laundry each day. mom didn't want her bath/jacuzzi tonight; just doesn't feel well. kristen will put a note on the log for tomorrow—bath! mom did ask to take me out to dinner tonight or tomorrow night; i had already said saturday night before she started this little dip. we'll see. her legs and feet seem good; any possibility of decreasing the lasix? she has had the urine in pants problem, big time. too much lasix? she seemed much stronger when i arrived on wednesday. today, quite a different story. she ate very little for lunch. i asked the kingston folk how we keep the room "cool," with the heat on. they suggested turn off all things . . . which i did. mom needs it ultra cool for her breathing. on the nicer days, i've opened the windows for fresh air. shopped for mom; she needed briefs and cough syrup. aunt barb called last night, cathy and ralph yesterday; we talked to nick on thursday. i talked, briefly, to daph yesterday, as well. does mom have the clothes she'll need for fall? will she need a humidifier in her room . . . for better breathing? called nance at work . . . dogs are just fine. that's about it. i'll add a bit more before i go. connect with you next week; i'll come back friday late afternoon; earlier if possible. remember, i go to detroit saturday all day and evening, staying overnight, do marianne and church, and return if mom's coming for sunday dinner. then it'll be three weeks till i can come again. i need to work and build up some cash reserves. at the moment, it's very busy. good pickings. lots of selection. need to log hours. however, if any emergency, i'm here in a flash! caroline doing well; our circle of friends being very helpful. she should get a clean bill of health by the end of the sixth week post-operation. that puts that declaration mid october. mom seems to enjoy "her table" of friends she dines with; i've enjoyed them too. there may be a belated birthday wish with this note, donna. i sure hope you use it!!! i'll add more later. hi, it's later. another laundry, more pee pants. we went to the last half of happy hour. (kingston always has a happy hour on fridays. entertainment and a wee drink. wonderful for the residents.) mom's not feeling well. we'll see what's up tomorrow. we had a quiet night. i read, listened to some tapes. mom slept. she's not well. i'm bummed out. feel so badly for mom.

September 28, 2002

in mom's room. she's sleeping in a chair. told me she had a bad night, but no details. complaining about her neck hurting. her cough is more frequent. gave her the last of her cough syrup last night, will buy more. listening to her cough—is it emphysema or just a cough? either way it seems a bit challenging. dangerous? got your "surprise" this morning, donna . . . parking for it is very convenient. the person that you are to contact is flexible. do what works best for you. you go, girl—and relax. then do it regularly! so that's it, pre-lunch. i have a feeling no outing today. overall mom is not feeling well. wearing out? wearing down? so worried, but i guess this is aging. ill health. talked to daph friday night. she misses mom. says she calls mom's room regularly but most of the time, no answer. i wonder if she'd ever come up? we could show her toledo. she could have time with all of us, and of course, prime time with mom. just a thought. it's a beautiful day today. caroline called to tell me of a "work to rule" situation at the border and a highway patrol blitz regarding speeding, this weekend. god knows what i'm in for going home. well, mom didn't want to go down for lunch! took her breathing treatment and off to bed. i just ran to krogers for cough syrup. god, she's not well. breathing labored, movement a struggle. i look at this room. it's such a nice place. you guys did a great job. it's cozy. i hope mom loves it here. gets to enjoy it for a long time. we'll see. today, i'm worried. concerned about mom.

October 10, 2002

catching up, catching up. when i saw mom this past weekend, as part of my "renaissance unity woman's conference" trip, it was a quickie. i didn't like what i saw. she hadn't slept well thursday night, i saw her friday around six. i stayed and watched a bit of tv with her. i could tell, i always can, that she was feeling low. so much medicine and the lasix causes her to pee throughout the night. it's such a vicious circle. she was quiet. i was tired. not a good combination for us. she knew i was going to detroit for all of saturday and sunday morning. she knew i'd drive back for dinner sunday. when i see her like this, i know it's a downhill thing. i feel something worse is coming. get so worried. it always affects me, deeply, when she gets weaker. she seems sad to me, more defeated. so damn hard to witness. looks beaten up by life. no fight in her. oh, mom. i just wrote her the kind of letter she'll hate. i was encouraging her to remember things . . . and tell me, so i'll never forget. she hates that kind of letter, from me. for starters, through the years, i must have heard the stories, or whatever, and i don't remember. then, when i'm ready, i want to know. so that's not right, either. it'll piss her off and that's ok. i feel better for asking. i'm remembering how great the woman's conference was. oprah was the keynote speaker . . . but all the speakers—julia butterfly hill, riane eisler, bell hooks, anne lamont—were stellar. marianne was mc and just delightful. the gospel choir from renaissance unity was there; it was the best, the best, the best. marianne was thrilled and excited, proud and rightly so. oprah was something else. just awesome. no notes. talked forever. did a question and answer thing. so generous. miss o. what a woman! but nobody, in my mind, outdoes marianne, who is blessed by god with her gift of intelligence, charisma, and performance. really, she is. marianne was stellar at church on the sunday after. i always, always benefit so much from her sermons . . . well, they are really just talks. not just talks, you know what i mean. i think marianne should be up for a nobel prize. she's been lecturing for about twenty years on peace and love, started a few charities of her own to help those with aids, feeding the hungry. she's moved, touched hundreds of thousands of souls. in the name of love. peace. she's worth a nomination, for sure. i'm remembering riane eisler from the conference; she has a plan for us to improve our behavior to work together. why doesn't she get more media attention? i don't get it. life, as it is, right now, i don't get it. we do have the answers. we can live together, in peace, in harmony, on this planet. some people actually know how we can achieve that! why don't they get more media coverage? riane's thing is the "partnership way." i encourage you to find her books. read. she sure is something! and before i get back to mom, marianne edited "imagine." a must book for you to read! we have the people, they have the knowledge. duh! but this is about mom. mom, you worry me. i guess i'm remembering riane and the partnership way, because it occurred to me that i started to get along with mom when i didn't allow her to boss me around anymore. i wanted to be equal. i vocalized. i pointed out "unfairness" when i experienced it. i became aware. we . . . mom and i . . . started to have more of a "partnership" than a dominance thing, by mom. it worked so much better. we became more peaceful with one another. amazing. this may be a key for you, the reader. about your relationship with a parent. well, after i returned from church on sunday in warren, i raced to donna's. we went to pick up mom for sunday dinner. it was a custom. on the way back to donna's we stopped at niece nance's new house. mom hadn't seen it. me neither. damn cute. keven, nance's beau, bought the house as an investment and rented it to nance. wonderful little home. mom enjoyed seeing it. then back to donna and ron's for dinner. good rib dinner. damn good. mom enjoys these sunday dinners . . . with family. it's a nice thing. i'm glad we, they, do it. i'm so happy when i can participate. mom was tired, didn't want to stay at all, after dinner. an eat and run thing. she seems much weaker. her breathing seems more labored. hard to witness. donna was encouraging mom to take a quick trip to chicago to see an estranged brother who isn't well. short history: mom got pissed off, shortly after dad passed, with her sister-in-law and brother, for not acknowledging, from mom's point of view, a more in-depth expression of sympathy. so for years now, they've been estranged. part of our family's insanity. one false move, you're off "the list." nobody knows what's on that list. oh god. i guess we're like all families but . . . i'm sorry for all involved as that was mom's kind of favorite brother. i can't say that. she loves all her brothers and sisters. but we had a lot of contact with these two. lived in the same town for a lot of years. now for the real insanity . . . then i didn't speak to my aunt or uncle for years . . . because of mom's "influence." not her influence exactly, but if mom did it, well, i guess i figured i had to do it. then one day, i just called them. then, when i was in the area, i saw them. i loved them. and love them. so mom was a bit pissed off with me, but got over it. i didn't influence her behavior. i simply had no reason for not connecting with them. at any rate, mom didn't want to go to chicago. she said she just couldn't go on another trip. granted, she's not in good shape. in this conversation with donna, about the proposed trip and refusal to go, mom comes out with, "and by the way, i know i'm not going to return to arizona either!" well, donna was floored. when she shared that with me, i was floored too. i can't remember where i was when that all went down. obviously, not there, as i would have pursued it. i have no idea what this all means. mom's thinking . . . she's passing? she's not healthy enough to go "home?" she's kidnapped? i can't imagine what feelings are in mom's heart, what's in her mind. i can't. i'm so sorry for old folks and their transitions out of their homes to nursing homes, from independence to dependence, from health to struggle. what a journey! i usually pause now and then when writing, even skip a few hours, or days, weeks. i don't know how long the pause was this time. i am so sad; affected by mom's statement. she thought she was coming for the summer; going back to arizona. after donna and ron's military reunion. what a bummer. what a bummer. i'm sorry mom. really, truly, i am. i cry as i write this. it just seems so unfair . . . not anyone's fault, no blame, just circumstances. mom's not felt well . . . i think, for years, really. this, that. a series of this and that. a gradual sink. depression. i don't think any old person should live alone. but what do you do? god, i don't know. it just seems so difficult for mom. unfair. why do i say that? she's suffered, whether it be from her own bad decisions, or whatever, enough. suffer is a funny word now that i write it. but when one is in agony, discomfort, lonely, not feeling well . . . when does it become suffering? i think mom suffered and is suffering. i think this is mom's road out. the toledo road. not how she wanted it. and possibly, her ride is here. it's sad. i really love my mom so much. i never realized how much until i started to write about her. i recommend this process to any and all reading this. record, record. an amazing process. get to your inner self. those thoughts, feelings, yearnings . . . that were buried in the family shit. the mother-daughter shit pile. any parent-child shit pile. these feelings are worth the digging up. so worth it. if you, the reader, are sad, i honor you. you're getting to the feelings that count. keep going! i think i am, you are lucky. we feel. i was afraid, for years. i was numbed out. numbed out. we're so lost for the most part. so hard.

i'll own it. i was so hard emotionally. i didn't and don't want to be that way. there is a rumi poem that reflects this exact feeling. i'm sure i've quoted it somewhere in this book. there is a line . . . about being hard. oh my, it's a powerful poem. i'll stand and say, i love my mom. stand up! say it! i can remember being angry at mom. yelling, screaming at her. of course, from afar. i remember times, i'd get off the phone with mom, slam that damn thing down and yell, "oh, i hate my mother!" and just sob. caroline would witness this, and help me process. what a fool. just a reaction. i never hated my mother. angry? upset? disappointed? many times. but hate? no. not hate. never hate. so much therapy. oh, so much therapy. now i'm laughing and smiling. what a spiral we go through. aren't we just so . . . strange? i am at a good place with mom. today. grateful. paid my money. paid my dues. have my voice. have me. i'm an adult. we are now two adults dealing with issues. a good feeling. not easy. not easy. i highly recommend it. dad is another book. took a lot of therapy. another time. so, i'm saying to you, the reader, keep processing. it's your foundation. your balance. your parent. when both are gone, or if you were raised by one, he/she goes, we're orphans. another process! heal as much as you can. i am doing that. i am. it's work. bloody hard work. takes guts. do it. please do it. for them. for you. for after. i have never felt so whole. i think much has to do with marianne williamson: her words, her tapes, and her books have been my motivation, to be bigger. you must find someone who speaks to you. of course, before marianne, there is god. but god is more silent unless you are actually lucky enough to hear a voice. i feel god; i've never heard him speak. but i feel he speaks to me through marianne, through amma, the holy woman from india. through other clergy. brent. through nature. through silence. i guess there is a language with god. for me, it's not a spoken language. it's a feeling language. i'm better with the word. i like to hear the word, encouraging words. so that's why i honor marianne so much. and a course in miracles. another take on the man, the energy, the source. i didn't connect with my sister the way i would have liked to this past weekend. she was fried from the military reunion. she worked hard on it. she's been in stress with mom, the reunion, just being a good mom herself, a grandmother, a daughter and i'm sure, a sister. a wife. a lot on her plate. i can remember my ride home was bittersweet. concern regarding mom. the war. (like marianne says, let's wage peace!) my life, as it is. so much to think about, to process, to improve. truly, improve. becoming a better person takes thinking, planning, action. you must want to be better. i want to be a better person, spiritually. and however that translates in all ways in my life. i like the image of me reaching up and holding god's hand. i never held my father's hand. seems sad to me. i can't remember being hugged either. sad. it just never happened to him, so how would he know how to hug? my dad had a challenging childhood and i'd say, a mean father. dad was not mean. stern sometimes, strict. never mean. if you were to talk to donna and then to me, i think you'd get two different takes on both mom and dad. that's life, isn't it; two people see, feel, experience two different ways. i know for me, i'm constantly reminding myself to hold god's hand. i can see it, feel it. i see the visual. it's so beautiful. calms me down. it does. so, here i am today. i am sitting in a cube van, driving for a camera crew on a feature called "highway man." we are out of the city quite a distance. it's still early morning and i'm freezing my ass off in this van. i don't run my engine to stay warm. it's not good environmentally. so i'm freezing. sun's up. when it's warmer, i'll stand in the sun. how lucky am i? get to be out in the country, interact with an interesting crew, and one of our greatest actors is in this . . . colm feore. he's good. i'll take a break now. the next time i'll see mom, barring any emergencies, is the weekend of october 25-26. that'll be three weeks. donna and ron will be off to chicago that weekend; donna has a courier nurse reunion. she's historic. santa fe railroad. so proud of her! i'm historic. first second city touring group, ever. chicago second city. i'm proud of me. damn. i was funny years ago. i'm pretty funny now, too. oh god, i'm so happy i'm working. i sure need the money. our union has warned us about a slowdown coming. it's extremely busy now. have a pretty big selection to choose from when called for work: truck, van, cube, cast, crew, equipment. a choice, that's great. i'm a pretty happy camper today. i'm holding god's hand. and so it is. god bless. god bless you, mom, today. oh god, i worry about my mom. please, be with her. really, please. god bless us all, whatever we are processing. i'm remembering a t-shirt slogan: "life's a bitch, and then we die." oh my god, that's so silly. things happen. we react. get a grip. four agreements. god. we have the tools. get with it. get a marianne tape. book. have a good one. you're capable of that!

October 29, 2002

it's been a while since my last diary entry. again, i write from "my" van; thinking of mom and all that has passed recently. i'm actually happy; mom seems "good" at the moment. don't get me wrong. still some labored breathing and, generally, all that was wrong still is. but, she seems happier; or did this past visit. she's joking with her pals at the dinner table, she loves going to the dining room to see them, to be with them. she seems to be "close" to two of the women; it's wonderful to experience and witness. oops, another day. i had a very busy day at work yesterday, no time to write. such is the business. today. very quiet. same show, different call. i'm driving the electric pickup. i transport whatever is needed from their big truck to the set. so far, they have everything. i'm comfortable, it's quiet. i love this pickup truck. i love days like this; long periods of time to myself. i write, i pray, i think, i stretch. i drink water so much more diligently. need lots of water. i am indeed, happy. i like the guys. very polite, fun, professional. love that. i find when i have time for what i mentioned, i do have a peaceful day. i need time. oh, do i need time. i like that i'm aging, i'm clear on what i need to be happy: prayer, silence, awareness of breathing. all important. we are on a day/night shoot. hours are bizarre, not good sleeping on this schedule. i can't sleep into the morning or early afternoon, even if i get to bed at 4, 5 or 6 a.m. i just am not built like that. i'm early to bed, early to rise. i'll be going to toledo for ten days soon; donna and ron go to germany to visit mike, sharon, and the kids. i'll watch the house and dogs; be with mom a lot. see nance and elizabeth. i love toledo: the parks, the mall by donna's, and i love kingston, where mom is. it's a bad time to be away from work as there is so much of it; but donna and ron are good to mom, i want to help them out. be there for mom too. i've stashed my money away . . . now almost two months ahead with savings. i also have money for personal bills, joint bills. i'm feeling ok. my goal is always three months ahead, so i'm close. with the world as it is, war looming, there may be a real slow down. i hope to work until i drive to toledo. i've been on this show for a few days. that's all it takes, on this kind of schedule, to feel like shit. i'm so tired and turned around. i don't get enough sleep on these day/night things. when on a show that goes into night shooting, it sucks. but you do it. the only good thing about night shooting is i get to listen to the art bell show or his replacement(s) on talk radio. he's the real alternative radio show with so much metaphysical and "other" information. really good. it's from midnight till 5 a.m. my kind of information. a lot of para-normal, which i am. very knowledgeable, interesting people are interviewed. wonderful information, sometimes upsetting. sometimes scary. really, so much going on that we don't know about, that's almost unbelievable and isn't covered in mainstream media. "must" radio for the caring, concerned, inquisitive soul. honest injun. that's a weird expression, isn't it? what the hell was the origin of that? i'm still joyful about mom. i have a picture in my mind, of her smiling. it's nice to have that image. not that often i've seen her smiling, now that i remember. i picture mom and her pals at the dining room table, laughing and having fun. very sweet. makes me smile! as i write from the truck, the sky is that wonderful fall sky. amazing clouds today . . . such color within the scattered clouds; a wild painting of white, rose, pink, and a light tinge of yellow. beautiful. thank you, god. thank you. i've switched to the electrics channel on the walkie, quieter than the transport channel. this is good; checked the call sheet and dinner is in thirty minutes. yum. i'm starving. shared my avocado sandwich with eli wallach today; i had to shuttle him and he noticed my sandwich. he's a doll. so i'm hungry! my plan about mom is to work a full week next week. a few days the following week. and off to toledo. oddly enough, amma, the holy woman from india, will be in the detroit area, at the same time. i'll get to see her a couple of times, catch marianne williamson at church . . . all while in the toledo area. very exciting. just popped a card in the mail to mom. i like to send her cards, letters, notes. she loves mail, she always has. looking ahead, might get a week of work in before american thanksgiving and a couple of weeks in december. that would be good financially. by then, we'll know what's up in the industry, in the world. who knows, maybe mom will even level out a bit. oh my, life and its challenges. come to think about it, i think nance and elizabeth wanted to take the dogs. that'll work for me. i did have a thrilling day yesterday, just being in eli wallach's company. he's a democrat, a man for peace. compassionate, caring, intelligent. we got along fine. i really do wish we americans would tackle the problem of why people seem to hate us, head-on. there are ways to dialogue and work through things. why can't we get from this notion to some kind of action? i think this is where marianne williamson and company should be invited to help. i remember a saying . . . "if a problem can be defined, it can be solved." hello. surely we can define all the problems of the world . . . and then . . . hello . . . solve them. how can people in the world go on killing one another just because someone is "different?" is it greed, power, money? hate? oh god, help us find another way. you know what? it is my problem! it is your problem, too. so friend, yes, you the reader, what the hell are you doing about it today? i think that's the only attitude that has a chance. your responsibility. and, mine. i carry stones in my pockets; one says: "the life you live is the lesson you

100

teach." pretty damn right on, if you ask me. the other one says, "devotion." we can be devoted to peace, honesty, compassion, common sense . . . oh, so many things. i don't know how you, me, how any of us can live without god right here, daily. we need to keep saying to god, "i'm available. use me." quite honestly, that's how i keep emerging into a better person. i do that. i feel the change. i am that change. i love the change. and it's constant. good luck to you. you can change. just be open to it. then, we change the world. i don't know why so many of us are/were afraid to use the term "god." it's like it's not said; except on sundays. god is important. change the name, if it doesn't work for you. the universe's energy is important. tap in. turn on. truly, god bless. god bless us all. use us. step up to the plate! it's time. i gotta eat. can't save the world when i'm hungry. honestly, you . . . me, we are the difference! later.

November 19, 2002

i last wrote october 29th. i was excited about mom, amma, marianne williamson. well, it was a time beyond my wildest dreams. i must say i'm much more into the "now." that really helps with "whatever is." no expectations, no attachments. whatever. by god, it's working. first went to amma; catching the end of the wednesday morning public program. it wasn't too crowded; several hundred people. manageable. how can i explain being in the presence of a saint? you enter a different realm of energy. and the smells . . . of india, incense, flowers, a hint of rose . . . so so good for the heart. i love good smells. india has a special smell. a spiritual smell. amma brings it. the music . . . all kinds . . . all spiritual. an india sound. live. tapes. good for the ears. good to hear spiritual music in the presence of a saint. you can feel the love. you can. i feel the love for amma, from and through everyone. i feel amma's love for all of us. it's very special. i feel sorry for those who haven't experienced, or if there, don't get it. maybe some don't. it's really deep. some folks don't let deep things in. that's too bad. if ever you have a chance to experience amma, please do. with an open heart. see what happens. you'll "feel" and that's an incredible thing. i got in line for darshan (the hug.) it was sweet to wait patiently, to pray, to look, to listen, to be. just to be. be in amma's presence. amma is very compassionate with each person, each couple, with the sick, the lame, the families. with everyone. i had a flower for amma; it's a good thing to give her something. later, it's all recycled. they sell any and all things at the "spiritual mall," as i call it, that travels with amma. all kinds of "amma" things. all sales go to help her charities, good works, deeds in india. elsewhere. she helps so many. even though you're not supposed to talk to amma, i do. my spiritual name is "jaysuda." amma's childhood name was "sudhamani." so i usually say " i'm jaysuda, you're sudhamani . . . we're the "sud" sisters. love you, ma." something like that. she smiles. laughs. gives me a good hug. then, holds me in front of her, looks at me. smiles. hugs me again. oh, it's delicious. she says to me, as she holds me and rocks me, "my daughter, my daughter." great. it's just great. she's something. i fill up with love. unconditional love. what a feeling! there are indian meals to buy, snacks, chai tea. mmm. yum. good. this past month, amma was the keynote speaker at the u.n. for the world conference of women religious and spiritual leaders. in addition, the most prestigious ghandi-king award for nonviolence was presented to her for humanitarian efforts throughout the world. only four given so far. the other three recipients were jane goodall, nelson mandela and kofi annan. amma. amma. what a living saint. then off to my own ma. she was in such a good mood! we talked, we laughed, enjoyed each other so much for two and a half days. my god, it was so much fun. so loving. i think the best visit ever! we had such tender moments like when we were watching television and she said, " it's so much nicer when you've got someone to share this with." i think we were laughing at funny home videos or something humorous on tv. it was the best. we had fun at her luncheon table with the gals. mom must have been lonely, i filled a hole or something. i felt appreciated. i'll take that super mood, for whatever reason. then headed back to amma for her last night, a public program. this time there were a few thousand at the hotel. the darshan numbers were past 3,000. the hall, hotel—jammed! all very well mannered, very pleasant atmosphere. i was in the welcoming crowd when amma arrived for the evening. put my hand out to be touched. it was. felt thrilling. i stayed for a few hours then headed to my motel to get a good sleep so i could enjoy church with marianne the following morning. no matter what subject marianne chooses to lecture on, it's meaningful to me. she simply has to be one of the best lecturers of our time. i've attended quite regularly since we relocated mom last march. warren, marianne and the church are about an hour and fifteen minutes from toledo . . . given good conditions . . . traffic, weather, speedsters, cops. again, marianne was simply stellar on dealing with a possible war. suggested we ask angels to protect our beings, our cities, our country. prayer is necessary. her latest book is just out, "everyday grace." she's been on a book tour. came back for sunday church. doing a bit more of the book tour right after. her energy is incredible. her body looks fabulous. she should put out a "how i stay fit and live like i do" book. she talks to any and all who line up to speak with her after service. available. a graceful, giving woman. an angel, really. i drove home touched by amma, my mom, and marianne. i was grateful, i cried a lot. how fortunate i am. how blessed, to have these experiences, to feel so much. blessed. i was motivated to think how i could change what i do to reflect a more spiritual persona, a deeper commitment to being a better person. it was fun, fun to think about that. i decided to definitely use my phone messages for spiritual tidbits, use my annual christmas letter for spiritual motivation and reflection. i'll deepen my coaching practice by having a more spiritual bent to it. that will happen with intent. who i am and continually become, is reflected in how i think and act. i will be changing. we do. constantly. that's if we are alive. it was all good thinking. exciting. can't wait to read marianne's book. i'll have to start going to her web site more. amma's too. many good things on the net. well, i'd better get it together and do some errands. i just wanted to catch up with my diary entry. what's good is i'm really getting it, regarding my own responsibility in my changing. nothing on this planet will change, until i change. become more loving. more daring. more vocal. more spiritual. more compassionate. more peaceful. more non-violent. so many things. life is exhausting. but damn good fun. and so it is. god bless. god bless your changes. i'm remembering an old 60's song. a woman sang it. "the changer and the changed." it was a good song. sometimes you hear a song, or remember one, that just says what you're thinking, feeling. those are good moments. today, i hope you have good thoughts, hear good music. god bless you, mom. it was such fun. you are such fun. god bless you, mom. god bless you all. and so it is.

December 2, 2002

was in toledo for thanksgiving dinner. stayed through sunday morning. left for warren, marianne, church. i arrived in toledo after a pretty good drive; clear roads, little traffic, easy border crossing. donna had already gone to get mom. ron was very hospitable; holiday happiness. yanks love thanksgiving. it's my favorite. when donna and mom pulled up, i went out to help unload. mom's feeling the cold weather; "get me in the house." she was in a good mood. yippee. we got settled, had a bit of holiday cheer. mom likes her bourbon. she's been off it, lately, but had one. i'm telling you, she was on an up. so great to experience. she sipped her drink, we talked. dinner wasn't till 5. donna and ron did what they had to regarding dinner, i entertained mom. nancy and elizabeth arrived. nance's boyfriend was still at "their" house working on kitchen cabinets. elizabeth and i had our connection, including mom in all of our conversation. the holiday phone calls started; family members calling to wish us all a happy holiday. it was nice. aunt barb, nephew nick, cousins called. we had a superb dinner. mom hasn't been eating well, but she chowed down. she doesn't like how she looks. she has put on some weight. the heaviest mom has been. i guess those steroids cause this. i think she looks good. honestly, i do. but she sure isn't happy with her looks. i think she's on a hunger strike, kind of, trying to lose weight. she's vain. mom's still got that hacking cough. awful to hear, can't imagine what it's like to have it. generally, she's hanging in there. oh there are the continuous urine, bowel accidents. no time to get to the toilet. sometimes she gets up before she's done. now that's a worry. sometimes she can't remember why the carpet is "dirty." perhaps the mind going? you just clean up what needs cleaning. period. then again, her mind is sharp on other things. now she's a cnn devotee. loves the split screen, all the information. and she'll comment on what's up. awesome. god bless mom. whatever phase we are in, god bless it. she's funny too. i'll ask her, when i remember, "mom, did you eat breakfast today?" she'll respond with, "i'm not answering on the grounds that might incriminate me." i laugh. so, she's with it, on some counts. god bless. i rubbed her feet on thanksgiving. it was a nice moment. friday after thanksgiving, we did the traditional get up early and shop thing. donna and i got started late, 7 a.m. what a crazy day. donna loves to shop. i'm fine not doing it, but this day, it's fun. we bought mom a fake christmas tree and a beautiful santa for her room. i stopped over at mom's for lunch. somehow that day or the next, i fit in the movie "frida." oh god, was that ever good. god bless you, salma hayek. and julie taymor. brilliant. brilliant. everything in it and about it. oh, frida. frida kahlo. her life. her pain. her darkness. amazing film. you know you've seen something special when the lights go up and no one moves. talks. at least for a few minutes. indeed, that happened. amazing. i love when i feel i'm better, my life is better, for experiencing a movie. indeed, that happened. i spent that friday night with mom; we watched america's funniest home videos. she loves that show. it's funny. we laugh and laugh. it's nice to do that together. saturday morning donna and i did some more shopping and then went to mom's to begin her christmas decorating. mom was in awe. her room took on such a wonderful, warm christmassy feeling. she was touched. mom and i had lunch. she rested afterwards, i went to donna and ron's for a bit. i came back to watch tv with mom, after her dinner. it was yet another wonderful evening. my god, i was happy. the room was darn cozy. back to donna and ron's to pack up for my warren trip early a.m. i usually get to church early; browse in their fantastic bookstore. i can't believe marianne's last service will be new year's eve. my god, how lucky was this church to have marianne for almost five years? man. i was surprised that marianne mentioned a few things at service today. it seems she's had threats, lots of unkind things happening, pressure to leave. what a bummer. i know she wants to stay until new year's eve. i e-mailed the church and board members when i got home. i don't get it. they can't work out the differences? but i'm not there, don't know the facts. there's always two sides to a story, but i'd have to side with marianne, if i had to choose, at this point. she is so loved. well, by the people who come to see her. her talks are brilliant, stirring, inspiring. such an angel. her book is on the bestseller list, already. "everyday grace." that's what she seems to embody. be. i can't thank her enough for helping me, helping my healing with mom. i will keep mom, marianne, the church, the board members, in my prayers. it's life, isn't it? there is light and darkness. it's all a part of the process. god bless us all. our lightness. our darkness. our challenges. god bless us. god bless mom. later.

December 28, 2002

it's been a long time since writing; i hate that. it's been too damn busy. caroline had to go to holland to visit her mom. the holiday season itself, is intense. running the house, taking care of the animals. juggling friends, family, spiritual practice. then too, i do adult sit michael when i can. it's been intense. post-cancer, aging, being low on the seniority list at work and financial challenge; i don't handle pressure well. i need things calm, planned, predictable; yes, i need to be in charge. hello! then life lets you know you're not. mom is bad again. and i'm here, alone with the dogs while caroline is in holland. damn. also, my computer . . . well, the e-mail sending and receiving died. just too old a system. i have no money set aside for a rainy day. the rainy days have been toledo, mom, back and forth. in fact, i cashed in most of my savings. so much travel, not enough work. foolish? well, the way i see it i need, i want to be there. not working that much, even though mom gives me nearly $200 every time i visit . . . i lose three times that (or more) each time. so i keep losing money. i'm not that focused on money; mom is more important than anything. mom is still here, i'm very low on funds, my computer system is just too old, and i'm embarrassed. i can live with that; my choice. i've asked my dear aunt barb for money, asked mom. if i get it fine, if i don't, well, when i get enough money together, i get a new computer. that's how i live. it's not like i'm not working; i'm coaching, as i can. i'm doing the sacred shopping, as i can. the film industry will be "up" the first week in january and yes, i'll call for work. so that's the information on that. boarded the dogs with our dog walker, ed. i drove monday, december 23 to toledo and returned december 26th. it was an awful few days. oh yes, we laughed on christmas eve; opening presents. mom, donna, ron, elizabeth, nancy, keven, jim, and sandy. it was hard to see mom again; she's not like she was. her bowel movements are pretty unpredictable; loose too. she's not eating, hardly at all. she has no energy, just seemed like she was slipping. i can always tell by the level of conversation and the look on her face as to how she's feeling. not good. to me, donna seems nonchalant about it all; although i think that's her defense and coping mechanism. i was sad going into the trip; hating to leave the dogs, hating christmas without caroline, a friend's daughter self-mutilated the saturday night before i left. that was terrible. generally, i feel sad and bad. i wanted to make marianne's service in warren, michigan, but couldn't. then there is the world situation, which is interwoven with each of our lives. calls for constant prayer, and visualization, and good intention. i was not in good shape. crying a lot. donna was on my case about that; we had words. we never do. mom cried a bit. before we went to church and at church. donna was careless with wheeling mom into church; i got mad at that. it was awful, really. i hate that donna doesn't encourage, allow, let mom process her sadness. well, i don't think she does. thank god we had comic relief with jim and sandy, on christmas eve. they are fun; and made the evening enjoyable. donna works her butt off. it's a challenge having mom right there. all in all, it's stressful. for donna. ron. all of us. christmas day was no great shakes. everyone low on energy; i had lunch with mom. she was tired. and sad. we didn't talk much. she was pretty quiet at donna and ron's. i played a little jr. scrabble with elizabeth; my god, the girl cheats! she's fun. smart. clever! we took mom back to kingston pretty early, cleaned up the dishes.

went to bed. ron watched tv. his back was "off." i was happy to leave; cried the whole way home. just exhaustion. emotional exhaustion. i'm removed from it all by five hours. it is what it is . . . but it's shit. that's hard to deal with, but one does. i am in no mood to socialize. will have a quiet and very prayerful new year's. i always make my new year's goals on december 31st. it's pretty easy. mom is the focus; take care of myself, work, and make as much money as possible. keep writing this journal. coach. i would love to have some fun . . . but it just doesn't seem right. oh, i have the odd laugh about something, but it feels heavy. and i'm too heavy, physically. i've got to eat and drink less, move more. it feels like a heavy time. the good news for me is marianne williamson will talk at church two sundays in february, and two in march. there is a new board at church. yahoo. it helps to have your spiritual leader available. she'll be in toronto, via the learning annex, at the end of march. god, i hope you all have your marianne; somehow, someplace. caroline is coming home in a few hours. she's returning with her niece. i'll take michael to church tomorrow morning; have lunch with rita and ingrid. that's comforting too. i'm on the edge. i feel it. i hate this place. the edge. i'll be ending this entry and do some spiritual reading before errands and the airport. i think i'll be having a good cry, too. i cry because mom is alive and not well. i'm sure going to cry when she goes. marianne has mentioned some group in japan that laughs when people die, cry when they are born. we do go home when we die. i do believe in a spirit, that energy that is a life force. it goes home. it's really such a friggin' mystery, but i choose to believe. i guess i still want it my way; more good times with mom. more sweet, gentle, kind moments. the odd conversation. less, so much less, struggle for her. everything seems to be slowly shutting down. she's a bit mixed up, more than she used to be. i cry about that too. damn, it's sad. if you are reading this and are on the same trip, with a parent, or someone, i'm sorry. i hope this diary, about what it's like for me, honestly, is somewhat comforting. to let you know you are not alone. you aren't. there are many of us, going through this. loving a parent. loving someone. wanting them to be at peace. be there. in some way, be there. sometimes silence is good. when there is nothing to say, silence is good. or holding a hand. or stroking a brow. or simply being there. being a witness. or pray. prayer is always good. god bless you. as this year ends, god bless you. do your best. be there. when someone needs you, or even if they don't, be there. god bless my mom. please god, be with my mom. and so it is.

January 8, 2003

it feels like the beginning of the end. writing in mom's room, toledo hospital, after lunch. i came yesterday, after a call from donna sharing, "well, it is serious." we had been talking since sunday night, when i knew something was not right. i had called mom's several times, no answer. i called donna and ron's several times, no answer. i just knew something was up. mom had constantly complained about not feeling well and finally donna and ron said, "well, we're going to emergency." they were in admitting from 4:30 p.m. till after midnight. poor mom; waiting, waiting, waiting. tested for many things; finally admitted but then had to wait for a bed. donna and ron got home at 2 a.m. test results showed basically it's deterioration of both lungs and heart. the emphysema is getting a bit worse. her congestive heart disease is escalating a bit. she's had chest pains and we were thinking possible heart attack. however, it seems to be angina; i guess one half of her heart is enlarged. the procedures that could help are too invasive at this time. then, there is a possible blood clot, but again the procedure is too invasive. it's all more complicated than this, this is what i understand. mom's slipping. bottom line. they are going to do one more chewing and digestive test; mom's having digestive problems. or a windpipe problem. there will be an evaluation on her physical ability too. oh god, i hope mom can return to kingston, but maybe she'll have to go on the catered side.

most likely from here she'll go back to lake park and have rehab there. the staff on second floor knows her well. and likes her. i guess one option is for mom to stay at lake park, which will be very expensive since mom takes so much medicine. at kingston, donna dispenses the pills and the aides make sure mom takes them. a huge savings. bottom line: safety and comfort for mom. she seems to slip, get weaker, recover but has lost a rung or two on the ladder. hard to witness. she's not eating well. she feels weak. she is. i feel badly for mom. she asked donna if she had cancer (yesterday). no one seems to think so; again, to go in and look, too invasive. we'd lose mom on the table. decisions. harsh and hard. mom feels sick. has that look like "oh no, i'm slipping and death is somewhere near." it's a look. donna seems worn out to me. seems bitter and short-tempered too. just worn out. i'm feeling quiet. terrible that i don't live here, but i can't help that. jesus, i wonder how long i'll be here. oh well, whatever. both mom and donna need me. it's always shocking to come into the situation again. this time, it's mom's eyes. they look sad and frightened at the same time. she is starting to have a certain look and stare . . . like she's beginning to see "over there." waiting. she's waiting. looking for the death angel. oh god, mom's just had a coughing fit that caused her to lean over and hold onto the bed railing. short of breath. crying. choking. i called the nurse; we re-adjusted mom. gave her some strong cough syrup. that's that damn emphysema. choking the lungs. she's calmer now. it's scary when you can't catch your breath. god, what happens when mom is alone when this happens? this is not good. oh god, what's going to happen? when? please don't let my mom suffer. i'll suffer. give it to me. don't let her suffer. please! mmm, where was i . . . i think i was thinking about kingston and the catered side. we'd have to insist on a salt-free diet. i don't know if they do that. a little thing like that is a big thing. you are what you eat. but i think no salt, or minimal, is good. there's another facility i've noticed, not as nice as kingston. we might have to explore that. maybe we'll have to rent mom's home, for income? oh, so many things pop into one's head. i think mom has another two years of money left; she could pull out of this. she's really enjoyable when she feels good. when i think of it, just keeping up with the medicine on a weekly basis is so much work. thank god for donna. at one point, i made a comment to donna about how we just don't seem to get a flow going with mom. a rhythm. mom has all these ups and downs. i felt donna was a bit sarcastic . . . saying "listen to your own messages," referring to my phone messages, usually spiritual in nature, usually a marianne quote. i didn't get it, really. and then she said, "duh, this is the flow." i just let it be. but it did ring true, this is the flow. no predictability. ever. in life. for mom. or now, for my life. i want some pity! i leave my home, my partner, my animals, my job, my income. my surroundings. donna's home. she's home with her partner. oh well, this seems to be my calling now; be here with mom. help donna however i can. and, get a grip! it's hard for donna; she has her way. i come and i ask a million questions; have my way. i'll just trust. i will. i guess i'll pray more. have to. just do what i can; for mom, donna, for me. let's see, what's up? my friends are good. my friend guylaine just called with a beautiful prayer. how timely was that! for the rest of the afternoon i'll do my marianne reading; always helps me. pray. scan the papers. watch cnn with no sound. i like doing that. it's like things are happening but i don't want to hear about it. damn it's cold in this room. mom is supposed to have it cooler because of the emphysema, but damn, i'm freezing. i'm sure i'm allergic to air conditioning. i sneeze to beat the band. camille, a speech therapist, is doing the swallow test with mom. seems painless. camille thinks mom may have a reflex disease known as gerd . . . wants to order an upper g.i. with barium but i don't think so. i insisted we wait to talk to donna. i don't know what's invasive or not at this point for mom. i don't know if mom has had this trouble for a while or not. i just talked to donna and she said mom does have the reflex disease . . . and i'm thinking . . . what, i didn't know that. jesus. where have i been? donna got a bit short with me, again. i think i'm irritating her. she's stressed. donna will talk with dr. wenzke. another doctor just came in. who's he? dr. tamirisa. mom's heart beats fast. but he's not that concerned because mom also has lung disease. they usually go in tandem. adding cortisone to mom's rotation? talking to donna about this. keeping an eye on mom's blood pressure. mom doesn't look well. i'm worried. wish donna was here. i'm no bloody good with all the new info, the search for answers on this intelligent planet. donna's a former nurse and works in the field. knows mom's history so well. i'm doing my best. god forbid when people have no support. oh mom, god bless you. oh mom, i'm so sorry. god, are you here?

January 10, 2003

here in the hospital, again, after a day from hell for mother. i thought she was going to die yesterday. she had a coughing fit that had "good-bye" written all over it. there were others too. the day started with a choking spell, then the ordering of an emergency swallow test. then going for the test, which was hurry up and wait, all the rooms and corridors were cool to cold. mom got very little attention during the long waits and was totally impatient; yelling, angry, mad at me, the whole bit. it was awful. she continued to cough throughout the day and evening. coughing and choking and gasping for air. i finally left at 8 p.m., when she calmed down a bit. at one point, she was so frightened, grabbing for the sides of the bed, hacking, gasping. awful. it was just bloody awful. those eyes of hers, looking for help. peace. comfort. tears in them. so bloody awful. she was simply miserable all day. i actually prayed for god to take mom. emphysema is so friggin' ugly. to watch, to witness. don't smoke. please don't. you will suffer if you get emphysema. mom needed help and there was none. there is none, folks, when you're choking. it's simply hell to watch. to try to help when you can't do a damn thing. i feel badly for mom. honestly, i thought she was going to choke to death; and that's pretty ugly to witness. death's doorstep. now that's a strange phrase. today? she's off the doorstep. thank god. i can't even remember when i stopped writing or started again. there's been a break in time. i can't keep my notes straight when this kind of thing happens. donna bathed mom at one point; i assisted. i went to the cafeteria at one point and x-ray and speech pathology came. things happen. you wait. you go for a moment, things happen. life. mom even sat up in a chair while an aide, heidi, changed mom's bed. i returned, donna left for errands. then mom wanted to go to the bathroom, didn't made it to the commode. there was shit and pee all over; smelled, bloody mess. so sad. mom feels awful when this happens. so friggin' degrading. oh well. we'll all have this experience. christ, when i had "the bag" (temporary colostomy) i was having accidents all the time. shit all over my bed and me. not great memories. i'm used to this, but not accustomed to it. it's an awful experience. at the same time as mom's accident, a woman fell in the next room. a true hospital moment. intense. patient down in one place, shit all over in another. mom is bloody heavy, i can't hold or move her alone. mind your backs; boy, donna and i have sore backs. it's hard work. be mindful of your body. mom was so mad at me; i couldn't move her, she wanted to return to bed; she's a mess, the bed and the floor are a mess. no one could come and help, right then, and mother's giving me shit. i couldn't do anything. i'm yelling, "hang on, hang on. there's an emergency in the next room with a patient down." mom's wanting help, now! she will stand for no less. i'm pleading with her, "mother, damn it. someone will come. just hold on. please." it was so bloody awful. someone did come. got her and everything cleaned up. this brings up my own cancer, shit, bag, survival issues. man, it's raw stuff. i look at the time; after 3, mom sleeping comfortably, it's a quiet moment. the room's been busy. the hospital is busy. pat, in bed one, just had a cancer of the colon operation. has a huge family (extended) and is receiving more and more visitors. and flowers. donna has left the building. i'll wait for the doctor to show, tell us about mom's x-ray. the new medication is very good. she's resting peacefully. coughing and hacking less. thank god. i don't think she has pneumonia. it's just that damn emphysema. i'm planning to leave tomorrow morning, after dropping by the hospital. that's if the doctor thinks it's an ok idea and donna puts her rubber stamp on it. hopefully clear weather and a smooth drive home. hopefully i can make it for "ducks" birthday and drop in; a dear friend. i'm so emotionally whacked. i need peace and quiet. i need to rest, in case there is work. there should be. i'll miss a transport committee meeting tomorrow; i hate that. oh well. i missed earning some money with michael, too. i need to earn money. i'll just trust that i will. i'm grateful for what is. i'm dozing off, better stop. i'm tired. i hate this feeling. not good for long distance driving. poor mom. she's tired. but she seems stable. 100% different than yesterday. guess it's the right medicine. the stomach guy was in; we'll do nothing. i think we're still (slightly) wondering . . . cancer of the stomach? you start to ask every question. everything is too invasive for mom's condition. if we did "invade" and "find;" what then? oh, mom. god bless you. you don't deserve to be this sick. just isn't fair. i'll sign off. i'm pissed off, with god. damn. now why's that? i don't understand suffering. my mom's. i don't. i think i'm holding him responsible. i'd better work this, pray through this. perhaps it has nothing to do with god. i've gotta think. later.

January 17, 2003

well, a lot has happened since the last entry. i'm at lake park rehab holding the fort for a while. donna and ron doing mom-related errands. mom is here to die as comfortably as possible. there, it's said. it's sad. she's fought hard and long, but she's so tired—exhausted—and so many things are going wrong. so best thing, let her be comfortable. when i left last saturday, i didn't know for how long. as it turned out, mom started slipping. it's been very hard on donna. she's been here nonstop. i figured i'd be here yesterday, unless needed before. i needed to go home; be with caroline and the animals, get different clothes organized for the funeral. i had a chance to take michael to church, and a movie to boot. "lord of the rings: two towers." was that ever good. but i felt tired, sad, worried. then the calls started; fast and furious. return as soon as possible; be prepared for anything. mom was pretty quiet saturday. then, i think on sunday, she started to go a bit downhill. that's been the direction. several things are happening; they discovered a problem with the esophagus, that's why the swallowing is so challenged. too much calcium in the blood, kidneys failing, a few other things i can't remember right now. all very negative. at one point someone suggested dialysis; donna said absolutely not. there was tube feeding thrown in; again, absolutely not. mom must have been awake for that one, as she said "no, no, no." the hospice nurse was in, talking to them both; mom was pretty out of it. it was decided to keep mom as comfortable as possible. we'll cut some of her medication, keep the catheter in, although mom is uncomfortable with it. it does the job. enables her to eat and drink; no worries. i guess wednesday before i came, mom was bad. then thursday, very bad. in fact, she was to be transferred back to lake park; i was to meet them there. i show up at lake park to the message "come to the hospital." i'm thinking she's dead; she died. holy fuck. i raced over there like a mad woman. i prayed and cried all the way from toronto for god to do his will. i couldn't believe it, i left home in such a hurry i left a friggin' suitcase! i was about an hour away from home; i called caroline, crying. i was so out of it. nervous about mom. it was the suitcase for arizona! as the universe would have it; i so needed that time to calm down for a safe drive. caroline, god bless her, without hesitation i might add, changes her schedule around. meets me with the suitcase. honestly, she is so generous, considerate, and compassionate. without hesitation she does these things. she's been so supportive of my journey with mom. i burst into her room at toledo hospital. she was out of it, but alive. she looked like she was dying. donna and ron were at her bedside. i just flat out asked, "what is up? she's dying, isn't she?" donna said, "you'll cry if i tell you" and i'm saying, " no, i won't." and she said, "yes, mom's dying." and yes, i cried. not too much, not hysterical. i just went into shock. you know it's going to happen or it's happening; but it's a shock. so, we're entering the final act. they didn't transfer her to lake park as the hospital thought she was dying too. they left mom to die. be as comfortable as possible. be at peace. can you believe it, she rallied a bit on thursday night! donna and i saw dr. wenzke friday morning; we were up and out before 6 a.m., at toledo hospital for 6:30 a.m., trying to catch dr. wenzke doing his rounds. we caught his associate and then the big guy himself. he's like tim robbins: tall, good looking and a pleasant manner. "comfort care" is all we can do. i'm numb. i wonder what's going on for mom? not too communicative. oh my god. the final act. i'm still numb. in shock. all i can do is pray. talk to god. please god, don't let mom suffer. take her. please god. be here, now. oh mom, love you so much. god bless you.

January 20, 2003

just past noon. at mom's bedside. a horrible past forty-eight hours. mom's still alive. we'll put her into a private room today. she's on morphine as needed, suppository for bladder spasms as needed, and something else once a day to move her bowels and relieve her gas. morphine can bind you up. i have knowledge of bad gas pains; with the cancer of the colon, the emergency operation, and the reconnective operation. oh my god. you think you're going to die with the gas buildup and no release. it's the worst. i'm convinced. anyone reading this; you may know that pain or if someone you know has it, please respect it. as horror. mom isn't eating, has had these horrible bladder spasms. mom just moaned, "oh god, help me." a familiar chant now. she's in such pain. often yells, "oh god, let me die." she looked over at me, in agony, crying, looking so pained, "oh, charlene." i called for the nurse, in tears. she's medicated and sleeping; it's 12:40. i'm sure we'll be changing the room shortly. it's hard to be in a twin, knowing death is coming. hard on the other person. not fair, really. god this is painful to witness. mom is the most miserable i've witnessed. i'm going in and out of crying, sobbing, myself. i'm not that strong in this situation. damn it's a miserable day. i really don't understand why mom has to suffer; to linger in this pain. she wants to die. this is truly an example of bad things happening to good people. why? god should take her. he should. this is the delicate part of trusting god; i think something should happen, but perhaps god is more in charge. duh? i guess there are no should's for god. i go back to my marianne williamson tape on letting go, asking god—can you take this situation, please? you handle it. that's what i'm asking. i guess i'm including "should." not good. god is handling it. i should trust that! it's between mom and god. i can only witness and pray for . . . what am i praying for? i'm praying for mom not to suffer, to die peacefully and to let go. maybe i'm praying for the wrong things. i need to think. god will do what god does. simple as that. all i can do is make sure mom knows i love her, that i'm sorry this is happening, and to encourage her to pray to, talk to god. she has to be in that communication. i can pray for a miracle. maybe the miracle is i let go? i can pray for mom to let go? is that valid? it's between god and mom. mom, let go? god, take her? that's between them. i pray that mom's in no pain, take the pain away. is that fair, god? god, i pray for you to guide me as to what the hell to pray for in this situation. i'm so confused. i'm using another good book today; another guylaine suggestion. she quoted a poem out of it, not long ago. i can't remember the poem, but the book is "talking to god" by naomi levy. i think she's jewish, as is marianne. jews, to me, are special. they are very compassionate and loving. they seem to have a good vibration in that area. higher than we anglos? perhaps. that's just the way i see them. i always say i'm jewish by desire. i can talk to god pretty easily, but i enjoy books like this. books of prayer. "illuminata," by marianne, is so special. i do think we should make up our own prayers, for the most part, but when stuck or lazy or confused, boy, these types of books sure help. you know me by now, marianne's the best. in every way. books, tapes, cd's, classes, lectures, but the best is marianne at church. check out her web site www.marianne.com— believe me, you'll thank me. i can't imagine knowing her. must be so special and yet, probably has its moments. she's human. mmm, i wonder. yes, i'd like to know her. i've been missing my dear friend suzanne bristow, who went to heaven, gee, a few years ago. i prayed for her to send me a sign; wanted to know if i was really communicating with her. damn, if i didn't get a sign. i was praying for sue to be ready for mom; welcome her. be ready for her so mom would feel safe and not afraid. damn if a picture of sue that had been missing for months, didn't fall out of some papers. i couldn't believe it! then a nurse "marianne" showed up! oh god, what a day. i felt in touch with the lord. and sue. and marianne. i took it as "just keep reading that marianne . . . and listening to her." as for sue, well, she is waiting for mom. i know that. i felt so damn good. that's what we do, isn't it? interpret things, things that happen, how we want. i trust that. intuition is soul energy, isn't it? it is! oh god, i haven't a clue when mom will pass. i just know i'll be hanging by her bedside until she does. oh god, i hope i'm with her. i don't want her to die alone. i know i don't want to die alone. i want a king-size bed full of friends, family, the animals, and some damn good scotch and/or wine. we're all yakkin' and listening to good spiritual music. and i slip away. happy. content. safe. ready. wouldn't that be nice? mom's eyes are doing this funny jerking, rolling, blank look thing. she looks lost. she looks up like she is seeing something unfamiliar. like she is dreading where she's going. it just seems strange. i don't like this look. eerie. oh . . . well, just be here and witness, touch and stroke mom, respond to any and all commands, demands, needs. exhausting but satisfying. it's mom, after all. it's mom. oh god, i trust you're here. i do. i trust sue is ready, up there. thanks sue. and marianne, i trust your energy is here with me. amma, too. that's good, for me. thanks. god, i have a lot to thank you for. the way i am. the way i feel. the way i think. i know you like me. i know it's ok to question you, question life, question suffering. thanks god. you let me be who i am. you love me the way i am. i feel it. so grateful, god. so grateful. i know you love my mom. she's been faithful and has done so many good things. take good care of her, god.

thanks for being here, now. thanks for whatever and however you're going to do things. i'll trust that. right now, in this moment, i'll trust that.

January 21, 2003

here with mom; another challenging, sad day. mom is uncomfortable when awake, which isn't that often. seems to sleep soundly when the drugs take effect. has that horrible bladder spasm, or something we don't know about, connected with urinating. she's mentioning a few more names of people who have died. talking about god; a little while ago she looked up at me and said, "it's just you, me, and god." then went back to sleep. she's had diarrhea, no fun. she's been spitting up quite a bit. can't seem to swallow or hold anything down. it's been a challenging day. her vitals are still pretty good. although she's bathed daily, to me, she's starting to have "a smell." add the chest rattle sound from the congested lungs and it's, well, it's dying, really. decay. donna said, "oh, that's the death rattle." well, that freaked me out. a lot of people get that, near their time. i've had a pretty tearful day; the past two days, in fact. donna, too. we've started to make lists, get a plan together. you know it's coming but somehow to actually experience the process, to get organized for it, is hard! there is a business about death. it's so emotional, yet you have to function on some rational level. weird. friggin' weird. sad. mostly sad. a horribly demanding profession—health care. all are very kind. still waiting for the doctor. it's 4:25 p.m. i was told about an hour ago he'd be here shortly. that pisses me off. that's another gem of a saying. duh. no patience when it comes to anything dealing with mom.

thank god mother has fallen into a deep sleep. she has no patience either. cut from the same cloth. mom goes in and out of sleep, deep sleep. when she's awake, she has that eye thing going; i call it "wandering eye." shortly after that, the pain comes and she's yelling, crying, or begging to die. man, is this sad. i could not be around this kind of "thing" as a job. boy these caregivers should be given lots of credit. i can't imagine when mom dies. we've got to get to arizona. honor her. lots to think about and do. thank god caroline has said all along she'll come to arizona. i'll need her. stan said he'll be coming too. from chicago. this is good. i'll be happy to have them both near me, near mom. i'm trying to remember things from a marianne tape. i'm so tired. i'm praying that i just surrender this situation to god. oh god, your will, your will . . . i'm giving this whole thing to you, god. surrender. i need to surrender. be ye as a little child. all i can do is be my best; be on my best behavior. i have no control. that's a hard one. i have no control. can't be attached to result, just live the process. i guess the bottom line is that we have to relax in the now; how else can god work with us, through us? his energy can't come through a stressed-out body now, can it? oh mom. please, please be talking to, praying to, god. give it over. he is in charge. god bless you, mom. god. please be here for mom. i think i'll shut my eyes a bit. pray. i'm feeling so sad.

January 22, 2003

sitting by mom's bedside and i'll be damned if she doesn't have this appearance of a native indian, to me. she has a very handsome face. totally native indian. beautiful. androgenous. just a beautiful native indian. it's her gray hair, her wrinkles, the way parts of her cheeks are sinking in. such a handsome indian. mom's hair is usually short, curled, well coiffed. but now it's long, straight, and going in all directions. beautiful. she looks like a great warrior. she is. for the amount of food and liquid she's putting in; i mean it's very little, like she's been on a hunger strike, she's doing ok. unbelievable but true. she wakes up now and then, can be very funny, and goes in and out of logic. just a while ago she wanted me to take the coupons and shop. make sure donna gave me money. before that it was, "oh, my lordy." last night before i left she belted out, "god, help me." i asked if she was in pain and could i help. her response, "no, it's just a saying." mom's sister, aunt barb, called suggesting we light a candle and pray the rosary. sends her love. she's a fine woman. she's been such a generous, loving aunt to the whole family, especially our family, especially me. she's bought a few of us new cars! she paid for my 2000 honda civic because "i'm alive," as in surviving cancer. sweet. sweet. sweet. mom's getting her second breathing treatment. donna says mom's pulse is getting weaker. oddly enough, we haven't talked about dying today. there's been a few opportunities, but we just let them go by. donna and i agreed to take the next one. we must talk about death with mom, make sure she's ok. if not, process some of it. what's an opportunity? well, this morning mom asked why she's not getting any medicine, "am i dying?" donna and i looked at one another and i think you have the instant or not. damn. we let it pass. i can't remember what donna said, "all the medicine was making you sick, mom. we just want you to be comfortable. are you?" mom said "yes," shaking her head in agreement. sometimes i don't know if mom is all here or not. it becomes a sensitive thing; figuring out what is up. i pray god is guiding us. our words, our actions, our hearts. i'm telling you, that marianne tape about letting go is helping me so much. she also has a "on death and dying" tape, which is very powerful. my god, that woman and her knowledge. so helpful in this situation. i'm laughing, remembering on the letting go tape, the audience is meditating, and a baby is crying out of control and loudly. marianne, at the end of the meditation says, "and god, about this baby . . ." so funny. the woman is funny. ah, another day of bearing witness to mom's journey. thank god i'm here. i feel so present and calm today. i guess i truly feel i have no control. it's a good feeling. just "be." i'm relaxing into that, finally. i feel better since they took mom's catheter out. she feels no more bladder spasms. much more calm. amazing. that damn thing was causing mom so much discomfort and pain. duh. thank god for dr. wenzke. last night he said, "let's take it out. see what happens." the mind boggles. i haven't felt good for a while; my god it's good to feel good. catching a bit of the australian open; i love tennis. am a pretty good player. love to participate in sports, generally. i sure miss swimming. i try to walk a bit here, but not near what i'm used to. mom loves watching the animal channel. that's weird as we've only had one pet in our family life, brownie, a wonderful dog, that we gave away. mom has a cardboard dog named lucky in arizona. i always laugh about that. i miss my dogs and cat. i love swimming with casey. oh, that is truly a wonderful feeling. sammie likes the water but doesn't swim out far. need to move more as i age. active. stay active. i have type o blood . . . and according to a blood type thing . . . we need a lot of exercise. i just know that resonates with me. when i'm active, i feel good. extremely good. donna and i sat here this morning. donna was telling me mom's history. mom is such a success! she left the farm (southern illinois) at thirteen, went to chicago to clean houses and do nanny work, with her sister. also worked in a meat packing factory. donna also told me the saddest story about mom's first communion. she studied for it but never took the host as she thought you had to have a white dress, which she didn't. mom came from an extremely poor situation. she and dad did really well. i'm so proud of them, but especially my mom. what a gal. amazing. i think i'm just going to look at mom, with pride, for a while. my indian mom. god bless her. later.

January 23, 2003

i don't know what's going on, feel unsure today. i need a marianne williamson tape. thinking about what is important in life: our goodness, our sense of purpose, a sense of meaning, our sense of moral justice? many thoughts; who we are in relationship to whomever? who am i in relationship to mom, right now? makes me think of feeling, purpose, behavior. who am i to the world? in the world around me? my actions, thoughts, and feelings reflect all of that. love thinking like this, about these things. you know, no matter what one believes, we are children of the creator. our sense of purpose should reflect that love. i was created as a total whole. i am everything. i can't be more. nothing can make me any better. it's when i/you, let my/your ego go astray. that's when magnificence is compromised. that's an amazing thought. oh, that ego. when i'm quiet, meditated, i'm so clear. i feel love. i look from my heart into mom's eyes; i see her. i feel so much love. that's it. boils down to that. not flowers, candy, teddy bears. marianne has a tape on something like this; touches upon this in a few lectures. the problem is we think we're not enough. but to god, we are a perfect creation. "he" is already pleased with us. god doesn't create junk! we work so hard at "becoming." just be. live. love is god. god is love. love is truth. i always wanted to talk to mom about stuff like this. she couldn't go there. god bless her. i'll just look at her; loving her in my truth. her truth. god's truth. my god, she is handsome. later.

January 26, 2003

my personal angel showed up today. i had misplaced, yet again, a favorite picture of my dear friend sue. alas, it falls out of some papers. i'm asking her to have a special event ready for mom; as that was sue's expertise. oh sue. what a gift you were. now, an amma picture has reappeared mysteriously. my, my. now all i need is the real marianne to walk through the door, and i'll have a heart attack. mom is going to be in good hands! i take these as signs. i never had closure with sue, which upset me. we talked a few days before she went into the hospital; we were to go to church together shortly before that. she didn't feel well enough. i can't emphasize enough about closure with a loved one. we should have a closure day, once a year. official. get together with loved ones. and have closure. and party. share the love. special cards and all. we should do these things when we're alive, people. in "moments" like these; finding lost pictures, connecting with someone special, a special moment with mom, whatever . . . something that has "special" attached . . . i cry easily. i think i cry more easily since the cancer. that woke me up! i'm thinking each day, this is it for mom. she dips, but then she rallies. often, when in a deep sleep, breathing like a last breath is coming, she awakens, is funny, and acts like "what's up?" oh my. last few days, when the "what up?" look and personality came through, there have been requests for krispy kreme doughnuts and milk, cheeseburger with onions, genoa salami on a hard roll. now mind you, it's a bite or two, max . . . but remember, mom has not been eating and has the swallow challenge. we're just going with whatever. she may die at any moment. let's keep her happy. last night, she was wide awake between naps. talking a blue streak with the nurse, the aide. she was even arguing with me about how she wanted this bed thing, with the tabletop, right by her bedside with the water on it. i didn't want to leave it like that with her shaky hands. she has no sense of balance or depth. and no strength. i lost. my last reminder, before leaving, "here's the tv/nurse call button and remember you push the red button for help." mom meanly replies, "i hate when you and donna tell me what to do." the mind boggles. the nurse and aide said, "go, she's in good hands." i left smiling and thinking, my god, she's back! then, this morning, when donna arrived early to help with her bath and breakfast, she observed that mom's back to where she was. she's quiet right now, resting peacefully. pretty much out of it. so, a new day. what lies ahead? donna's thought this morning was that maybe we should get an airbus and fly her home to die. i agreed. we'll investigate; cost being a factor but we'll see. her condition is bad. she may not be able to travel. everything has happened pretty damn fast since mom's been here. man this is all such a surprise. mom's health. ill-health. so fast. i had a great crying spell on the drive over; npr station was playing john williams movie music. beautiful. beauty encourages me to cry. just feel it. like communion. love the movies. the music from "e.t." is so good; and because i do believe in aliens, well, i just feel that music in a special way. steven spielberg. what a guy he is. i guess the part of "e.t." that gets me, deeply, is "e.t. phone home." i know mom wants to go home badly. it is painful. she even said to dr. wenzke, "i'd love to go home, but i don't think i can make it. god's in charge. that's all i have to say." i cried when i heard that. i'm here into my eleventh day, bedside, with donna. drained. sad. calm and grateful, to be with mom, at the end of her journey. what an honor. i can't believe the strength, as mr. bush would say, the resolve. i think that's the one word he re-invented during his presidency. my biggest learning is "letting go." being detached, in the moment, being mindful. being fully present. fully present. the journey continues. the lessons presented. and so it is. talk to you later.

January 27, 2003

it's 12:15 p.m. at mom's bedside. she looks sad today. she's sleeping now; ate a bit of soup, a few bites of fruit, eight ounces of grapefruit juice. donna left 11:30 ish. god knows what's ahead this week. i'm . . . what? so tired, for starters. i swear mom was near death again; i was grieving and mourning. then, this miraculous turnaround; perhaps a last hurrah? it feels like when i didn't get a film grant to do my first short film; being so stunned. i was devastated when that happened. i was dead; i literally died. beyond sad. beyond disappointed. horrible memory. i was ready for mom to go. we got to that point, and no, she didn't. stunned. just stunned. i talked about this with donna today. she's stunned too. it's a temporary upswing, we're sure. so, we keep the vigil. keep providing mom with anything she needs, wants, desires. call us the jump girls. why not? i sure want this kind of care when i'm in this position. we keep an approximate 7:30 a.m. to 11 p.m. schedule. we split it fairly. donna usually does 7:30 a.m. till 10:30 a.m., i'm here 10:30 or 11:00 till dinner. donna and ron visit before their dinner; i go out for a walk or do something. i'm back at around six. i don't mind. watch tv, hold hands with mom, jump when she stirs, read, listen to tapes, pray. bear witness. it's ok. sometimes i leave at 10 p.m. now it seems like keeping company and not the deathwatch. changes all the time. the likelihood of our being here when mom dies is 50/50. oh god, please let me be here. i want to be. i've split in the afternoon a few times; donna urging me "go to a movie." i love the movies. since i'm deprived of the things i love by being here, i go. i saw "the hours" and "the 25th hour." what theme do we have running here, charlene? oh my, hours. oh my. i was so depressed already, and then to witness "the hours," oh my. i knew it was brilliant, but i was numb. will have to see it again. back on my theme song; i just don't want mom to suffer. bottom line. who wants a loved one to suffer? she's weak. very weak. sleeps a lot. eating a bit more. the swallow thing? gone again. rev. bernice king, as in martin's daughter, is at renaissance unity this friday night. dare i even think of going? don't think so. want to so badly. mom, can't leave mom, i don't think. marianne is on this sunday. oh god. how can i miss that? that's my cereal. i've alerted donna about both. we'll be in the moment. then, too, there is the weather. if i make it to one or the other, or both . . . certainly worth the drive. in the moment, girl. my lesson. be here, now, with mom. i do miss home, desperately. just leave what you love . . . for a while . . . then you can measure how much you love it. i love my home, my life, my routine, my everything, so much. when separated from it . . . i go bananas. we're a day away from bush's state of the union address. mmm. oh my, we need peace on the planet, good communicators, good communication. most of all, good hearts! got to work as a global community if indeed we're fighting a war on terrorism. i don't get that the u. s. doesn't get this. check out the global renaissance alliance. they are doing so much for peace on the planet. www.renaissancealliance.org. back congressman dennis kucinch's proposed department of peace. www.dopcampaign.org. we've got the minds, folks. we've got the minds! the plans. the people. hello! so goes today. thoughts on everything. mom, spiritual support, life, peace, home. love. and the greatest of these is love. duh! oh mom. peace be with you. hope you feel the love today. hope there is no pain. just peace. joy. love. god bless you, mom. we're here for you. all of us. god, too. god's here. well, going to just sit for a while. be quiet. feeling so much. thank you, god. and god bless us all.

January 29, 2003

yesterday was a bad day. mom and i talked about fear of dying. mom said she wasn't afraid. she wanted to make sure i was getting enough money from donna. mom gives me money when i come; sometimes a lot, sometimes not that much. the bottom line is, she's very generous. talked with either cousin darlene or cousin kerin yesterday; i'm so mixed up and tired. i shared i thought for sure mom was going soon. that was yesterday. today, she's living. talked with stan from chicago; wants caroline and i to save memorial day, we'll do something special. wants to plan "it." something to look forward to. i'm using a lot of mom's lotions. my hands feel soft. they're often hard; crack easily. i've got my dad's hands. mom kept asking for the doctor yesterday. she had those ultra sad eyes. she moved her bowels; pretty normal. few urines. my niece nance came and did her toenails. mom shared she thought she was going to die soon. was fine with that. i'm by mom's bedside. she's sleeping, deeply. seems to be in pain today. we gave and are giving her full doses of morphine, as prescribed. no cries for awhile. after the high of the weekend . . . then these lows. such a roller coaster. yesterday donna called and she even thought mom was going. ron and i raced over. no exit. then, a bit of a rally in the late afternoon and evening. i had such a good cry with caroline on the phone. this is emotionally exhausting and so on the edge. you never know when the last breath is coming. what a strange thing; here, gone.

that fast. i'm praying to beat the band. that's a strange saying, too. but i am. it's mom's journey and agenda, not mine. and god's. i get off track so easily with my own shit. the ego, eh? not a good friend, at best. truly. i've cried about that already this morning; mom's journey and needs versus my ego and wanting things in my time. how insensitive. i need to keep singing that jann arden song. she's helped. her music. i remember crying a lot when i had the temporary colostomy. the bad accidents. crying about how horrible it was to have that damn bag. crying, wanting, clearly wanting, to live. "just" live. i think that's how mom feels. she wants to live. she's not afraid to die, but really wants to live. i've been there. i can understand that. if she wants to live, i'm going to pray for whatever she wants. and god, if mom is confused, talk to her. don't let her live in false hopes or dreams. what does god want? does god want? or is he just . . . just god. with no wanting. just lets us be? i don't know. he takes? we let go? right place, wrong time? i'm going back to just being. no head shit. going to breathe for a few moments and clear. back. here. here, now. empty. that's good. empty is good. i run out of patience quickly, want to lead my own life. ego. well, i'm here for mom's life, right now. so charlene, buckle down. we can abandon "the one in need" so quickly. with a thought, we do that. it's a bit embarrassing. this day, mother, i am yours! mom looks tired. her sounds are coming back; sounds of pain, discomfort. and she's short, as in, she made these sounds not too long ago and i asked, "mom, what's wrong?" sometimes she has a volume and a voice that is so off-putting. she responds, "nothing. leave me alone!" and yet, she'll continue to moan and groan. now, depending on one's mood, that comment can muster up the pillow over the face response. sometimes i just smile, shake my head; sometimes i leave the room with a tear, sometimes i leave the room with a "fuck you" under my breath. sometimes, i think—the pillow! it's always different. it's hard as i am 100% sure she does not mean to be rude or mean. she is in discomfort. that's discomfort and pain talking. i need to smudge the room, smudge mom. oh yes, smudge me. i often go to a place, when that happens, like i need to get outta here. be with caroline, friends, be outside. i need to go home. it's a momentary thing. ego. that's all. i often imagine god, marianne, or amma in the room with me. helps my thinking. my response to things. it's fun having imaginary friends. but they're not imaginary. i can understand why kids go to a place like that; creating friends. bottom line, i just want to sob. mom's suffering. it's not pretty. charlene, just bear witness. clear. be empty. be here, now. pray. and continue to ask, "mom, you ok?" no matter what response comes. i'm starting to say, "mom, it's your journey. i'm here to support you. i love you. i wish i could help in some way. i do. you let me know if i can." she gets it. i know she gets it. thank you, god. and everyone else who is here. in my heart. thank you. we're all needed. i need you all. thank you.

February 3, 2003

dying. the act of dying is not pretty. it's been a helluva journey these past few days. i thought mom was dying a few times. she's not dead yet. in some ways, i don't think she is dying. at this moment, she's sleeping soundly. it's 1:40 p.m.; donna and ron are off doing errands. i'm here, watching the coverage on columbia: the search for the answers on cnn. i'm thinking—that's familiar—the search for answers! foremost, what a tragedy that was. oh, how sad. how deeply this hits us all. i think we invest a part of ourselves in heroes, like those folks. support them. we're proud of them. we know them; on some level, we really know them. how inspirational they all were. what the hell happened? the search for answers. mom, what's up with your search? what does she need to know, so it can end for her? need to get? to experience? lets' go back to yesterday. i arrived after my morning in warren, michigan with marianne. needed to fill up my spiritual tank. glad i had a full tank because at one point, when mom and i were alone, mom just cried and cried, praying out loud to god, to mary, to please help her, please let her be well, one more day . . . to be healthy . . . crying, praying, repeating that message. "why can't i be well, please help me." oh my, we were both crying hard. i suggested that mom ask god to "please be with you." maybe asking to be well was too much. to be healthy. but then, why not a miracle? we were both praying, asking, talking, crying. at one point mom's breathing was so slow i called the nurse to look at her. mom got angry with me. she makes noises: grunts, groans. her breathing can change. i panic. i don't know what's happening. then she started crying again because "you hover so much, just leave me alone!" i madly recited the four agreements to myself. ask don miguel ruiz to shape shift and come on in. i need help here. mom pushes my buttons when i'm trying to help. all right, i hover. she gets angry. alert to the reader, you have to find exactly how to be with the person who is sick and/or dying. it's a hard thing to find; the balance. don't give up if you get shit. don't give up! thank god i had a full tank! all this happens in a moment; then i muster up, "i'm concerned about you mother, and i love you. i'm trying to do my best." the nurse came in, calmed mom down, calmed me down. then mom wanted popcorn. good, i'll go to the cafeteria. get outta here. before i left the room, mom reached for my hand and was holding and squeezing it. i knew it was her way of saying i'm sorry. i smiled. it was my way of saying it's ok, mom. it's ok. very emotional exchange. we had this look going. a window. i went in. "i don't know if you can be well, mom. but if you think you can, maybe you can. maybe there can be a miracle. but you have to move a bit mom. that's going to be extremely hard, as you haven't moved in a while. but you are strong willed, have a lot of courage, and i can't think of any reason for you not to try." mom kept looking at me, so i felt i could go on. "i think we're at a crossroads here, mom. you know you were really sick. you couldn't swallow things, couldn't keep things down. they suggested tube feeding, you refused. the doctor, donna, and i took that as an entry into comfort care. they also thought your kidneys were failing and suggested dialysis. donna and i, with the doctor, agreed that would be too hard on your system. we've stopped all testing on you, mom. no more invasions. we took all the pills away. we're trying to keep you comfortable. now mom, i think, and this is just my thought, i don't think you want to die. i really don't. it seems as if god isn't taking you either. so we're . . . you're at this crossroads. maybe we should get you moving. you've got to eat more. keep that food down. drink more. if you feel this is right for you, mom, do it! do it! let's see what happens." my mom has selective hearing. did she hear all of this? most of it? some of it? i think she heard all of it. granted there had been an atmosphere of "you're dying." but i think now we're going to have to support mom in "you're trying." i mean, maybe when you . . .when you're right there . . . nose in death . . . you say . . . i did say . . . with the cancer . . . i want to live! mind you, i was younger and healthier than mom is at this moment. but if mom wants to live . . . damn it, live! mom just held my hand and looked at me. she does respect me when i'm honest. i know that. that's if i speak quietly, slowly, and mindfully. not my aries rant. i think in mom's slow dying process, she's had time to think, a lot. thus rises the spirit of survival. living as fully as she can. as she is capable of. i think at one point mom just wanted quiet. i went for popcorn. nothing else was said. i shared with donna what had happened. i like being on the same page. so much happens so often, one does have to make an effort to keep the other up to speed. we're going to be proactive in talking to mom this week about being more active, eating more, drinking more. see what happens. we're going to try to get her to talk. mom doesn't share easily. talk about what's going on; death, dying, living, trying. not easy. not easy at all. that's no reason to not try. and try again. donna and i are to attend a patient consult this thursday at 10:00 a.m.; good timing for what's going on with mom. we're regrouping. donna will go to kingston to check out the catered side, we'll attend the consult, and we're talking with the doctor. we'll try to get everyone on the same page. amazing. the whole energy about everything is shifting. mom's even had a shower today; not an easy task for the marys—two aides who are so great. she's out like a light. i've been writing off and on . . . i don't even know the day, the time. it's like a new everything. walked through some new portal! she even had a bit of egg yolk and ham this a.m. had some soup at one point—feeding herself! shaky but did ok. i guess we're going for it! she continued eating at lunch—bits of cottage cheese, fruit, and a bite of key lime pie. and my god, a sip of coffee. i mean bits and bites. but folks, she's showing she wants to live. by god, that's my mom! well, i've made a promise to myself. i'll stay until mom's birthday, which is feb. 14th. by then we should know what's up or what direction we're really going. know how good mom's energy and drive is. so, a newness. a freshness. all moment to moment. it's all good. we've got a plan. and so it is! i love my mom so much. want what she wants. what a trip. you know, i look around these halls. life is fragile. vulnerable. i'm so moved by it all. often dying is not easy. not pretty. not predictable. it just is what it is. i do hope, by my sharing this, it will help someone. somehow. be with your dying parent. do your very best. be with someone . . . anyone . . . in a way you would hope someone would be with you. that's it. that's simply it. the hours, days, weeks, months—challenging on all levels. sometimes the moments of total joy are truly, just moments. it's love. you feel it. it's spiritual. be prepared. you learn. from the inside you learn. you deal with your heart in a way you've never dealt with it before. you'll lose your spiritual footing now and then. you get up again. much stronger. you go back to your sources and resources. you'll find new ones. you grow. you become a better person. you do. no one loses here, folks. no one. i urge you to give, to love, to be there. to serve. not pretty. not easy. but my god, and by god, you'll never feel so much, in so many ways. you do become who you are meant to be. by serving. by giving. i have to stop now. i'm tired. in many ways. that's good too. i feel mom and i went to a new level. that feels good. thank you, god. thank you. god bless you all. love you, mom. behind you 100%, girl.

February 4, 2003

watching the tribute memorial for the astronauts; moving. mom is not that good today. not that good. lots of sleeping and tylenol; lots. it's cold, damp, windy. generally, a dull, dark day. when mom was awake for her meal, she ate. even fed herself. she ate all the soup, bits of chicken and potato pie. had some cut-up peach. drank a container of lemonade. now she's out like a light. we need to move her a bit; she has to move. i guess first, the eating. she's still expressing a desire to be healthy! so the energy from the food may be what it takes. i'm pulling for her. she eats, she sleeps. she expresses a desire. all positive. i mean, she's feeding herself; that's fantastic. she'll have to transfer, which means out of bed onto the commode or into the wheelchair. that'll be a stretch. she's definitely in the zone of "i'm not dying!" i don't think her time is up. i think she's going to really give it a go. i don't know what to think. about anything. we've got a weekend decision about her room at kingston to make; keep paying rent? investigate catered side? do long-term care here? oh, bloody hell. this is difficult. what's difficult to project is how she will be. depends on her abilities, health, willingness, god. she does not seem to be dying now. but, no illusions, she is not well. my game plan is to stay until her birthday, then most likely go home for a few weeks. catch up on my life. then too; all depends. i have an important physical to take on the 24th of february; for my union job. i need to get my money together for march; which means i need to get some days, preferably weeks, of work. i'm not in a panic yet, but concerned. i have some money; juggling. i'm coming to the bottom of my barrel, though. just about a bare cupboard. the worst—financial concern. i'm truly trying to apply spiritual principles to my condition right now. be with mom. let go, let god. i guess i want to see a physical miracle. mom's now eating. that's one. if she can move, how great would that be? i turn it over to you, god. i do. mom is in your hands. i don't regret this time, i don't. or the money worry. or missing home. i may write that i do, now and then, but truly, i'm so happy to be with my mom. i need to be here. i want to be here. i love my mom. it'll all work out. and so it is. thank you, god. you and mom, you guys be a team, ok? trust you, god. i do. thanks again.

February 6, 2003

today i'm remembering that mom came to toledo with the promise of a return to arizona. it was to be a few months. for the summer, possibly fall. donna and ron would return with her. they'd have to work out "the dog." mom didn't want the dog in the house. now she's been to lake park, i can't remember how often! then back to kingston, room 222. such a nice room. nice place. mom was enjoying it. never got into a rhythm, though. always interrupted by ill health. damn. well, she'll not see room 222 again; maybe the catered side. that's if she's able to leave here. just imagine . . . not feeling well and bingo . . . downhill. it must be pretty bleak from mom's perspective. ah, so fragile, sensitive, with all these old and frail folk. what a damn hard passage for them. imagine losing one's grip. and for any and all children, holding on, but you see, feel, the person you are holding onto slip. more and more. i can see the visual. man. so difficult. for everyone involved. we thought mom was dying, yet again. her strength, resolve, will to live muster up another rally. i can't believe how mom's done on "comfort care." remarkably well. perhaps all old people, especially my mom, are on too god damn many pills! we're a friggin' pill nation. i think mom is on comfort-plus now. she's up a notch. she's hanging on, hanging in. another burst of energy. "help me get healthy" is her mantra. she's so damn funny, nice, enjoyable when she's feeling good. you'd be charmed by my mom. it can only be a moment or two, but, she'll charm you. we've had so much care and support up to this point—so appreciative of caretakers, aides, nurses, doctors... at kingston, lake park, toledo hospital. especially at lake park. they've taken care of mom like a family member. donna and i have been good daughters; we have. my god, the last few weeks... between us... i bet we've logged nearly eighteen hours a day. we love our mom. i will go back to toronto after mom's birthday... her 85th... god bless her. we're praying for a miracle. more movement. mom to get minimal therapy, gain some strength. she's trying to feed herself. improving. she'll increase her arm and hand strength, maybe even develop some leg strength. we're hoping she'll sit up more. that's challenging at the moment, but she gets a lot of assistance to do this. god forbid, transfer? (bed to chair... bed to commode.) my god, we're praying for big miracles. mom wants them too. donna and i will, god willing, start to spend a bit less time here. she seems to be heading into a healthier period and we feel, by giving her a bit of space to work with all the support here, she'll do a bit better. judgment call. god willing. please. please support mom in her efforts. god's will be done. i'm not sure about god's will. i'm really not. i think god created the world... created man... and i think said, with all the love in his heart... good luck. we are to do the best we can. i'm not sure god has much to do with all this. i've had too much time! thinking. pondering. i am confused. does god "take us" or "do we let go" or is it just circumstantial? i need to talk at great lengths about this. god, this is when i wish i knew marianne williamson better. i'd love to talk with her about all this. oh well, one day. donna's only like ten minutes from here. i'm five hours. with the stepping back, mom stepping up; we're close. i'll come back, often. oh god, if comfort-plus works, maybe mom will be happy. i'd love to feel she is happy. she hasn't been in such a long time. just that; feel happy. i can't imagine this part of the journey. the point where you are sinking... but don't want to sink. oh god, what a terrible ordeal. my only wish is that whoever is in that moment, is surrounded by loving people; family, friends, and caretakers who care. where do we get the energy for "the fight?" i know i got mine from god. mom's digging deep; she must be getting hers from god. there have been moments . . . one particular i'm remembering now . . . where mom said, "get me outta here." i said, as gently and with as much heart as i could, "mom, you've got to try harder. i'm so sorry. but you've got to try harder." we talked about what she had to do. the conversation ended with "i will." i love my mom. she's something else. i think after remembering that, after this entry of memories, i gotta go. feel like crying. crying for mom. for what she's going through. crying about so much i don't understand. crying that comfort-care plus works. that it's supporting her with a bit more medicine, going for it with mini-physio, encouraging her to move more. i know mom feels challenged. i know we all do. but god, i know she's in your hands. your love. how can that be bad? it can't. i let go, let god. i will pray for mom, to be the best she can be. right now. and i pray that mom has a good relationship with you, god. let her understand her journey. hell, let me in on that information too! i'm done for today. thank you god. god bless you, mom.

February 9, 2003

past few days a blur. mom's health is so up and down. mostly down. just intense. mid-afternoon. tired. if mom had a double bed, i'd jump in. emotionally tired. mom is crying a lot. she's sad, worried. she's tired of being sick. truth is, she seems much better than she was; which is a miracle. she's like on zero pills! amazing. perhaps it's the break from the pills that's causing all this; something better happening. she now gets lasix, perhaps one other, and the odd tylenol. compared to the shit load of pills before; amazing. she's had therapy today; arm and leg movements, and sat up for about seven minutes. friggin' miracle. she's eating well; by herself! i do think i'll have a heart attack if she walks again. however, we are on the miracle path. she just may do it, folks. she cried very hard last night; tired of being sick. she wanted to know if she's ever getting out of here. i felt so bad for her. we did move her out of her kingston room; we figured why pay for it if she's not returning to it. when, if she does return to kingston, it wouldn't be that room. it was depressing for donna, ron, and i to do it. i'm sure mom felt terrible too. she trusts us; but i'm sure that was a blow to her psyche. we put a lot of stuff in storage. donna talked to mom, a lot, about this. i kept telling mom, "we are going to move your stuff." i know there was more attached to the conversation, we wanted her to know. not be secretive. again, a judgment call. mom wanted to talk to us yesterday. i guess the conversation really didn't take place; she was getting her brief changed and we all thought mom knew we were leaving. she claims she didn't know. claims we didn't tell her we're moving her stuff. she didn't know where we went, or why. this is all upon return, when she's yelling at us. about leaving her. about moving her. ron left in a huff. donna, too. they wanted me to go, but i wouldn't. i stood my ground with mom, "i'm not buying into mom's manners. i'll stick around." i knew she felt bad. about the whole thing. why wouldn't she? but then, she's so money conscious. we thought she totally understood, knew it was happening, and when. she lost arizona, now she lost kingston. fuck. i mean, fuck. i felt so bad. for all of us. she was dying. now, it appears, she's coming back from near death. now, she's homeless. oh shit. i know we were quiet for the longest time. and there were tears, from both of us. i was crying for and about everything. i really saw the strain on donna's face today; in her body. i saw the stress between donna and ron. i cried for that, too. mostly, i cried for mom. in never-never land. dying but not. moved to toledo but now, no home, really. i cried because i was sure we all were doing good things; the right things. yet, all this sadness. damn. it was such a bad few hours. i wanna go home. oh man. mom is trying. big picture, doing much better. total picture, doctor says don't get that excited. did mom understand? i'm sure she did, in her better moments. maybe the reality of it all? i don't know. will mom trust us anymore? is this just a moment? now i'm in the middle. not siding with anyone. is there a side? i feel i understand mom a bit better than donna, than donna and ron. although they are here, i may spend a different kind of time with mom. perhaps we all need more patience. oh god, help us all get through this. i feel so bad for my mom, right now. maybe she just doesn't understand what's up. we'll create the nicest "home" for her, once we know where she'll be. the best. we want her to be safe, well cared for. oh mom. i'm sorry if we hurt you. so sorry. oh, this is a bad day. i see donna being pulled apart . . . she's a daughter, a wife, a sister. donna is very stressed. i hope mom sees and feels our love, from all of us. i'm glad i stayed. it's still pretty quiet. i know we'll talk when it's right. it just may not be right for a while. for me, this is simply the worst day. oh mom, i'm sorry you're hurt, angry, disappointed . . . i'm sure all those things. most of all, i'm sorry you are sick, mom. oh god, i wish i had a magic wand. to give you a day, a week, a month, a year . . . whatever god allows . . . for you to feel good. to laugh and smile. enjoy. i wish i had one, mom. i don't. my wand is my heart. it's filled with love for you, my dear mother. and now, i'll just sit with that. i'm going to pray for god to help you understand what we did. pray to god for you to remember we shared. we've not lied, mom. to pray to god for you to know we're behind you. we're for you. we all love you, mom. and so it is. i can't write anymore. i just can't.

February 10, 2003

mom sat on the commode earlier; very difficult and uncomfortable. didn't want occupational therapy but agreed for them to return near lunchtime. she sat up and ate her meal; basically unassisted! she was up a good twenty minutes, ate half the chicken salad croissant, all the coleslaw, one big strawberry, and drank two apple juices. her vitals are good. she's complaining of being cold. still pretty quiet since yesterday. everyone's walking on eggshells. a friend of mine called around two; we had such a great conversation. mom comments . . . i'm crazy or nuts . . . the way i talk. she said it in such a mean way. that really pushes my buttons . . . that she doesn't get me, my spiritual journey, my goodness, my life. all i did was stare right back at her, with the same meanness. then i said, "you have really hurt my feelings." i left the room. i cried, i went to the chapel. i prayed the rosary. intentions—try to understand my mom, not to lose my patience, accept that i'm very tired. stressed. can lose it easily. pray for mom. it's been a bad few days. prayed for mother to soften. oh i was hurt. i'm back in the room. there's tension in the air. mom and i aren't speaking. that's ok. at around 3:30 mom starts crying. she's really crying. i ask, " mom, why are you crying?" she snaps back, "please shut up, ok?" oh, i'm bloody pissed. but i breathe. and like a good croatian, i continue to talk. i explain about me, about the way i talk. i put in my request that if she can't say anything nice, don't say anything at all. i ask is she still crying about yesterday? "is the crying about your health? you are so much better, mom." there is no response. i don't know what's up. physical therapy is in the room! thank god. i'm outta here for a while. she doesn't want to sit in the chair, maybe tomorrow. she's wanting something done about a tray thing on her walker. don't know what she's talking about, but i have no patience. i leave. when dinner arrives, she sweetly says, "aren't you going to stay and eat dinner?" i wanted to get out of there, do errands, air out, cry, yell, scream. i excuse myself . . . donna and ron are there. that's still pretty tender, too. i'll be back soon, i alert all. i exit. don't know what's wrong with me today. when mom hurts me . . . i collapse. it takes a long time for me to pump up my own heart and soul again. i need time. i guess we all need time. i hope and pray we'll all get back on track. the air is pretty thick. oh, mom. i think you're hurt from yesterday. why shouldn't you be? i need a vodka martini! i need to walk and talk with god. marianne, where the hell are you? amma, amma. come on. all you guys. let's go walking. it's a bad snowday out, but hell, let's go walking. later.

February 11, 2003

mom seems to be retreating today. no talking. that cold air about her. i hate this persona of mom. she evidently vomited last night after i left. i didn't like hearing that. she's not well, again. and then, that emotional downhill spiral for her; closing her room at kingston, my sticking up for myself. damn. she's already had a crying jag this morning. no talking. damn. talked to the social worker. tried to explain what happened. maybe it's our fault for moving her. then i chatted with dr. wenzke before he came into the room. shared it's been a time. emotionally. maybe he could talk to her. then in the room i said, in front of mom, "mom seems depressed to me, and isn't talking. maybe she's angry with us, me or maybe she's confused on how good she's doing. can you talk to her?" mom shot me a look to kill. i left the room but stayed right at the door, out of sight. it took about five seconds for mom to start crying, very hard. i think her first comments were "i'm not getting out of here, not going home, am i?" it was tender. dr. wenzke said he didn't think so. he thought she was doing better, but probably not up to travel. maybe trying to remember, remembering arizona, was called for. it was all said with such sweetness. not like a doomsday thing. and as for getting out of here, well, her condition is not all that great. in order for her to have some quality, she'd have to move. get moving. get stronger. it was a lengthy conversation. i was crying, at the door. i went in. dr. wenzke suggested an antidepressant. still sticking with comfort care. mom was pretty quiet the rest of the day. i shared everything with donna. mom sat up for lunch; ate a little chicken, little potato, bits of bread and two apple juice. mother was quiet all afternoon. stayed in bed for dinner. donna brought a special dish from home. mom liked it. mom still quiet. we're not speaking. i'm feeling badly. i'm too stubborn to begin any conversation, but am alert, tending to any need. i'm planning mom's birthday in my mind. want it to be a special day. february 14th. christ. it all seems like a mess. at one point mom woke up from a bad dream. she won't share anything other than "it was a bad dream." now that scares me. don't know what that's about. late afternoon she did a little physical therapy, sat on the side of the bed. when they left, mom started complaining she didn't like the therapist's voice. "i can't work with someone i don't like." the social worker came in. i left. maybe mom would share some stuff. i caught up with the social worker later; nothing shared. i urged her to keep trying. she said she will try to get mom to talk. there was a disaster with mom and the commode, at one point. an unfamiliar aide was not as gentle as mom needs. mom started yelling, was livid! "you can't treat people like this!" a few of us calmed mom down. mother's skin is so sensitive to any touch. poor mom. mother shared with the aide, mary . . . "the bad dreams are about al." that's all she said. maybe we'll get more information. i hope so. she's coughing now. poor thing. what a bad stretch this is. her arms are so bruised from that last transfer. mom's almost untouchable. this is a friggin' mess. not good. i want mom to feel some encouragement. how would i feel if i had heard the things she did from dr. wenzke? how would i feel if i were having bad dreams? no home? man, this sucks. i know my mother always, always told us she never, ever wanted to go into a nursing home. well, we never would put her there, but she's heading towards a nursing unit. here? kingston? damn. damn. oh mom, i'm so sorry this is your journey. damn you, god. can't you help my mom get better? take her in her sleep, peacefully. do something nice! damn you, god. oh i'm tired. i feel so guilty. why? i'm overtired. confused. how can i damn god? help me understand, god. that's what you can do. talk to me. help me, please. this is not the picture i had in mind, for mom's final year, years. i need some silence. i'm not balanced right now. god, i do need you. help me with my perceptions here. help me. please help my mom, god. christ almighty, she doesn't need bad dreams on top of all this other shit. please, god. please, help us all.

February 12, 2003

when i called before leaving donna's, to check in with donna in mom's room, mom was alert and wanted to talk to me. "where are you? what did you do this morning? see you soon? love you, honey girl." honestly, tears. just bawling as i hung up. thank god, the darkness has ended! mom. mom. for whatever reason, thank god, she's back. that's the journey. that's the mystery. just go with it. when mom acts or is so tender, it just knocks me for a loop. it's like the mom i've always wanted. oh i thank god, even for a moment. thank you, god. when i arrive mom has been bathed, brief changed, eaten a good breakfast, and was napping. she had been in a good mood! donna and i left the room for the cafeteria; a rare moment together, alone. sister time. i love that. all too rare. i love my sister so much. we couldn't believe mom's mood. we sure loved that it had changed. we shared nurse and aide gossip. just life stuff. one of mom's favorite aides had a terrible background story. a friend betrayed her. when mom heard the story firsthand, with donna, mom's comment was, "is that bitch still here?" donna and i just roared. i laughed till i cried. that's our mom. so funny, so caustic. back in the room. mom wanted to hold a rosary today. that's fine. i was a bit alarmed; first time that's been requested. i had a good cry after talking with dr. wenzke today. no reason. it's just that mom is heading down the death road and it's so sad to watch; witness it. as the day wore on, mom was in discomfort.

started to cry . . . "oh, my back hurts ..." and then, "oh, my legs hurt." the nurse gave her tylenol. she slept. i was watching cnn, no sound. love that. i like it quiet for mom. some stupid suspicious truck is on a new york bridge. now what the hell is happening? some alert about a north korea nuclear crisis . . . what? all this and i'm preparing to go home. oh christ. what a world. mom woke up from another bad dream . . . crying. she did say it was "a bad dream." i ask, "you want to share anything about it, mama?" i get the look. i know she doesn't. she's having these bad dreams about daddy. that's all she'll say. i wish i knew more. her cough seems worse to me. poor thing. her arms still look like shit; that bruised look. her skin is so thin. she bruises easily. at least we're over those horrible, dark few days. i don't believe we've brought anything up. that's so like us; we never re-hash, review. god, i'm still encouraging you to work with mom on these dreams. please. give her some slack. she couldn't have been that bad in previous lives. don't really know, but don't think so. she sure is good in this one. please god, no more bad dreams. well, mom's up and i'll just be here, now. hopefully, we'll talk a bit. god bless my mom. later.

FEBRUARY 13, 2003

mom had a shower today! donna even rolled her hair. she got on the commode, with mary and donna's help. gently. sat up a bit in the chair. did some physiotherapy in bed. ate well. chose her own menu for tomorrow. slept. she ate lunch on the side of the bed, for me. mary, one of the aides, brought in hot dogs from home, with special chili sauce. mom ate one. she's eating well today. we had some family pictures in the room and mom suggested we rummage through them. she saw one of dad that made her cry. wants it laminated. she finally shared a bit about the dreams she was having. dad seemed to be doing something bad or mean. that was the bit. don't know much else. i talked to her about dreams. i shared the few things i think i've learned from caroline. share my perception of carl jung and his dream work. bit too much for mom. but she listened. hope it helped ease her mind. i suggested she pray to god for some further understanding and clarity. i know she won't talk to anyone, so why not the big guy? she's sleeping now. i'm planning a big day for her, tomorrow. i had suggested to my sister that i take mom's birthday party on. donna said go for it. and i am. donna and ron do so much all the time. i want it to be very special. i've gone overboard, but heck, it's mom. she's eighty-five. she's alive. and damn, i love her so. hope it all works. god, special invitation to you. please come. hell, you're all invited!

February 14, 2003

yippee! mom's eighty-fifth! she sat up for about two hours! she ate ribs, a few fries, veggies and dip (just a bit). sipped a beer. she's had so many presents, cards, phone calls. the room is filled with flowers, balloons, big valentine's ribbon, candy for everyone, candy for mom, doughnuts. i've got a big cake for later and champagne. some of the kingston staff said they'd stop by. it's been as festive, fun, and joy-filled as one can imagine. mom's so happy. really. she is. we did good. i did good. tonight, pizza and beer. mom's favorite. i mean, she eats a piece or two . . . and has a few sips of beer. god forbid, at one point the cake and champagne. perhaps a bit much. oh well, it's just the idea of it all. don't have to eat or drink. it's been a blast of a day so far. physical therapy even brought her up a tiara to wear. she's getting off on that! everyone stopping in, stopping by. she's in rare form today. seems to be feeling good, or pretending. perhaps i went overboard, but what's overboard? mom. eighty-five. dying. deserving! so, no holds barred. donna, though, did make a sarcastic comment to me. something about throwing the party i always wanted, never had. well, i just let it be. she's overtired. stressed. to me, she seemed a bit negative about this day. maybe she wanted to do things. she was welcome to. oh well. i did want it to be beyond mom's wildest dreams. i think it is. it's more than just a day. it's a remarkable day. eighty-five. she's never had a great party. not that i can remember. i'm hanging in there, with my joy, for mother. i'm thrilled with this day. i'm feeling mom is very happy with each little thing. and that makes her very, very happy, as there are many!

February 24, 2003

i've been home ten days—my god it feels good. donna and i are in constant touch about mom; by phone and e-mail. mom's having highs and lows. i still get alarmed when she's not well. she had to have another cortisone shot on her right shoulder, the shoulder where she had two (i think) rotator cuff operations. and bad arthritis. it's pretty constant pain for her; especially with the cold and rain. mom's amazing, responds well to the cortisone. she can now feed herself with a bit more ease; she's right-handed. i haven't heard anything regarding her crying or bad dreams about dad; i hope they've settled. whatever they were, my god, they were upsetting her. mom had a day of loose bowels and vomiting. worrisome. i'm told that it was a flu bug. with the current toledo weather, i can understand flu bugs and colds. it's amazing that there are so few colds amidst the caretaking team. really. mom is liking the occupational and physical therapists; she's doing ok. she has no mobility on her own, as of this moment. needs complete assistance. what a trooper. unfortunately, i don't think she'll ever get the strength she needs to do anything on her own. feeds herself in bed, but the cutting of anything is a challenge. i don't think she'll ever have control of her bowels again, or urine. god bless her; sometimes when she's really feeling great, that's not that often, she'll ask to get on the commode. it's never fast enough. in the health care system, you ring your buzzer, and wait. it's the intention that counts. mom has that intention. the attendants change briefs; pretty on top of keeping people clean and dry. i can't believe how normal it seems to see mom in a brief . . . dare i say, diaper? no one uses that term. we're all heading there. it's freaky, isn't it? that's one hard part of this whole journey, seeing where we are heading. jesus. live now. live today. do whatever you desire to do, today. i'm telling you. i am. for sure mom will go to the catered side of kingston. that is, unless they evaluate her and she'll require too much care. then that would mean lake park nursing. it's called something else, but that's what it means. we'll have an idea, just an idea, when i visit march 13-16th. it'll be a heads up for us; if it's kingston, we'll have to decorate the room, floor to ceiling. if lake park, we'll have to do very little. we're good with making things cozy; pictures, plants, flowers, some well-thought-out knickknacks. i'm sorry you missed 222; donna and ron did a stellar job. nance helped a bit, too. it was sweet. she will miss the staff at kingston and her friends there. "her table" at kingston is self-destructing. charlotte's up in catered, which is good as that's where mom could be, and they like each other a lot. new friends at that age . . . so good, isn't it? they could eat together. dorothy, another great woman from the table, "may be going up." they are monitoring her health and challenges. bad back pain. phylis will try another assisted living facility, just to see if she can do it. good for her! she's talkative and good for that table. there can be unbearable silence at the table, as i remember. people in their own worlds of thought. funny, as that's a good social time. doris, a delightful elegant woman, has already moved. there's a few "newer members", which mom didn't get to know. now that i'm writing this, i see so much of mom in me. not all things. but i do see a lot of things. mom does love the staff at kingston. and the staff loves her. she would see them, and charlotte, for sure. we could arrange for dorothy to come up, or charlotte and mom to go down, occasionally. it's not a common practice, but, hopefully, soft rules. in talking to some of my friends about mom, while home now, i do remember one very profound thing, mom shape-shifting into this very handsome androgynous native indian. to me, through my eyes. i was joking with her, calling her my mother cochise. i meant it. very handsome. mom's long, wavy grey hair and her wrinkled aged skin. attractive and distinct. her bone structure so defined. so native indian. i swear. she has a pained expression, too, that ages her. gives her a distant, historic look; worn out from battles that were hard fought and lost. courageous but defeated, tired. amazing looking; that's my mom. i don't think i'll get that vision out of my mind's eye. it was hard leaving this last time. i remember mom's birthday, every moment. what a great day she had. cards, flowers, balloons, visitors, wore a tiara from occupational therapy, ron's ribs for lunch, calls from family, pizza and beer for dinner, and a sip of champagne when the kingston crew were there. so many laughs. pictures taken. surrounded by family. at the end of the night, a major, and i mean major, vomit to end it all. remember, she does not eat that much, but on her birthday, oh my. after the vomit and clean up; i mean we had a bucketful, folks, then nancy said, "grandma, there aren't too many eighty-five year olds who party till they puke. cool." we all laughed. i think mom smiled. at that moment, she didn't feel too good. i was the last to leave. wanted to make sure she was calm. ok. and she was. what a day. i returned to donna and ron's to pack, had a drink, a bit of a read, some praying and sleep. an excited sleep; as i had been gone a month and two days. oh, i missed home. i process things "after the fact." it takes me time. time to feel. i remember once, in the 70's i think, i was at esalen, in a workshop on feeling of some sort. i was crying hard, expressing my sorrow about how difficult it was to feel, feel anything. i've come a long way, baby! now, i'm working on my timing! i was thinking of that "stonelike" image and remember that fantastic rumi poem my dear friend guylaine pointed out to me. i rushed out and bought the book it was in. it's become one of my favorites. read for yourself. from coleman barks, "the soul of rumi."

A Necessary Autumn Inside Each

You and I have spoken all these words, but as for the way we have to go, words
are no preparation.
There is no getting ready, other than grace. My faults
have stayed hidden. One might call that a preparation!
I have one small drop
of knowing in my soul. Let it dissolve in your ocean.
There are so many threats to it.
Inside each of us, there's a continual autumn. Our leaves
fall and are blown out
over the water. A crow sits in the blackened limbs and talks
about what's gone. Then
your generosity returns: spring, moisture, intelligence, the
scent of hyacinth and rose
and cypress. Joseph is back! And if you don't feel in
yourself the freshness of
Joseph, be Jacob! Weep and then smile. Don't pretend to
know
something you haven't experienced.
There's a necessary dying, and then Jesus is breathing again.
Very little grows on jagged
rock. Be ground. Be crumbled, so wildflowers will come up
where you are. You've been
stony for too many years. Try something different. Surrender.

isn't that just too grand? one of the greatest. for me. i think of surrender. surrender to moms process. just surrender. hard for an "in charge" gal. give it up charlene, past disappointments, resentments, past whatevers. past. it's past. just be here. now. oh

. . . eckhardt tolle. he's got it. man, he's got it. the power of now. you know, i'm learning, when i am in the now, it's so damn beautiful. you hear, see, touch, smell, taste . . . oh so deeply. it's like slow motion. you are touched by life . . . the essence of life . . . the breathing of life, because you can be. i'm thinking of mom now, in this moment, my handsome mom, who, when i left, was quiet after a great day. i remember just looking at her, feeling the happy, loving energy of that room. looking around and seeing the material expressions of love for her. it was all so alive. love was alive. mom was sleeping, but alive. she had pleasure. it was safe to go home. i was so alive, with mom. no more stone. turning into stone. i surrendered. my god. thank you.

March 11, 2003

it is sometimes challenging to sit and write; life. life's things. earning money, finding peace, praying for peace, juggling family, friends, the world. but alas, today i vowed . . . nothing else till i record my thoughts. so hello. as a writer i wonder who i'm talking to when i write . . . perhaps myself. that's ok. then i really like you. maybe i talk to god, and that's something i want to consider today. writing may be like recorded prayer; think about it. i do want mom to have painless, fearless, gentle days. i actually pray on that, for that. daily. i think it's important to record that. god, hello. i talk to you so often in the day, but like a partner, lover, friend, one can't talk too much. so here i am again, with thoughts on mom. my god, you were there with this last miracle. she was almost gone. now she's in good spirits, doing some therapy, eating some, moving. a bit. it's just unbelievable to me. i do consider this a miracle. i'm wondering, though, why are you not taking her or why is she still hanging on? is that how it works . . . you take us? is that the meaning of "it's our time?" predestined? no negotiation? it's not mom's time . . . no matter how bad she gets? she was crying a lot, about dreams of dad. you know my thoughts on that. no intervention? my take on the dream thing is she is processing old hurtful, sorrowful, painful shit about dad. she won't talk about it. now she's on antidepressants, so she'll not be able to talk about it. seems we do that here, on earth. we medicate. god, if she doesn't process this, will she be able to let go? does "letting go" enter into this? maybe that's our human perception and has nothing to do with anything. you see, it's confusing. i'm confused. i'm hoping you talk to me about this god; you know i'm dying for this conversation. well, not dying, but you know. i'm grateful. i am. mom seems in good spirits. she's had no real problems since i left, february 15. i'm returning thursday. a day or two shy of not seeing her for four weeks. i can't let it go much longer than that. i don't like to. guilt, in a way. she's only five bloody hours away. it is still winter. i hate the long highway drive, i do. now gas is so bloody high with the impending war. i think this is an amazing time, god. is this our finest hour? duh? is this the big test? you gave us free will and brother, down to the moment. we could have the most devastating war ever, but, we rally! awesome. you must be looking through your binoculars, chuckling. i hope you're thinking "damn good," "right-on" "duh, finally!" i do think we're good, in our hearts. i guess some hearts have been damaged. so damaged. that is where hate, evil, no regard . . . enter the picture? it's a time god, it's a time. traveling to the u.s., crossing the border . . . i'm not scared but cautious. i am more "alert." i thank you, god, for being with me, when i travel. for the connection i have, with mom. my connection with myself. with you. i've worked on this. still working. i thank you for the special people you've sent here. the ones i've found. you've sent some good souls. how do you elevate them? how do you pick your angels? who gets to channel sacred material? i want in . . . if there are any auditions. i do. i feel you have something to do with this diary. it's a good idea. why not come through me, with some material? come on. trust me. i do hope this book will encourage others dealing with a dying parent to open up more, to forgive, to love more easily, to pray more. be at ease. let go. there's a lot to figure in when this is happening. i think most of us need to be reminded. i needed reminding about many things; most of all, that i'm your child. spiritually and sacredly, your child.

i reflect your light. your light goes through me. when that happens, i feel so good. i hope some people can identify with that. mom, for being such a devout catholic, doesn't seem that spiritual to me. she has held onto her rosary more these past few months. she did want to have the statue of mary where she could see it. perhaps you're coming through. that's good. pray? i don't know if she does. i sure hope you and she are talking. she does get communion, that's good. i am anxious to see my mama. i realize more and more how much i will miss her. my god, what a strong woman. she's had a life. a hard one. too hard. i hope you are extra kind to her when she arrives. yeah . . . i do. oh god, i sure hope you're on top of her plan. you've got so many things to be on top of. are you sure you are on top of mom's plan? catherine roycht? please. just review it. update it. please, for me. i'll owe you one. thank you, god. i know you know i am coming from my heart. i know you know i love you and trust you. it's not easy for me, for a lot of us. you're a mystery! the biggest mystery going. but you know, i believe. thanks, god. thank you. god bless my mom. thanks.

March 17, 2003

i'm remembering holding hands with mom, on saturday night, during the last hour of my visit to toledo, at lake park. she was in good spirits. i love those moments—holding hands. such a loving exchange; no words, soft and gentle feeling, secure and honest, a moment to remember. hands and fingers move, remembering the years, the good and the bad, ah . . . the memories, the affection both passive and present. total connection. the length of time varies, but when it happens, and for however long, it's about as tender and sweet an exchange one can imagine. it's thank you, for everything, for all the time. it's good-bye . . . we never know, do we? be safe, be fearless, be painless. it's total love. it's powerful. those moments. i'll hang onto them forever. those moments make my trip worthwhile; the time, leaving home and all my connections, the money i lose at work, the inconvenience. it's all worth it, for those moments. read this over again, please. i encourage you to seek that kind of moment with your mom, dad, whomever. seek and ye shall find. i left, this trip, in winter. i'm returning in spring; so it seems. i left in peace, so to speak. i return in war. i left feeling pretty good and i return feeling sad, affected by the world we live in, by how we are as human beings. i worry once the bombs start, what will the repercussions be? will i ever get to toledo again? see mom? will there be a terror attack on u.s. soil, and if so, where? maybe in canada? all we can do is pray. we can do more! how about faxing, calling your government officials with your opinions? meet with friends and family in "circles" and discuss, pray, share information, feelings, action! we all have to pray for "another way." pray for change in loveless hearts to loving hearts, from senseless acts to sensible behavior, pray for miracles! as marianne always says, "we ask for too little." she was superb in church, yesterday. warren, michigan. check her web site! i believe it's time for a stronger united nations. a strong international community. i don't believe that the u.s., britain, spain, australia are that community. it's part of it. i know mom watches the news. she always has cnn on now. doesn't say much. but she knows; she listens, has opinions. i love her for that. mom and i are dyed-in-the-wool democrats. ron is ex-military, so hawk republican. donna is a common-sense republican. we just don't go "there" as a family. which is a lesson in itself, isn't it? well, that's no bloody good is it . . . if we can't even listen to each other? problem is, we don't hear each other . . . we're so stuck in opinion, tradition, party lines. well, better put this on the list to work on. i'm a dove for sure, but not a soft dove. a risk-taking dove. i am of the "let's look at all the perspectives" dove. i'm trying to be more and more open to "what will work." i'm all for pushing one's buttons, exploring boundaries, reasons, but surely one for law. laws are not made to be broken, but with reason, changed, for sure. one for justice, or again, exploring justice . . . and seeing if that's right the way it exists. funny, i can't remember being overtly influenced by mother or dad. but they were democrats. i can't remember anything, especially politics, being discussed. mom only had an eighth grade education. dad too, but he went to night school to get his high school diploma. my god, i'm so proud of them both. to me, they were very educated! they accomplished a hell of a lot. i guess i was more influenced by my catholic friends in college, by the 60's, period. what a time. i loved that decade. so loved that decade. i think i remain an old hippie, i really do. it's an important day for mom, today. she's being evaluated by kingston regarding whether she'll be ok in catered or if she'll be needing care above and beyond their capabilities. her biggest medical challenge, and it's big, is her skin breakdown; such sensitive skin. it tears easily. isn't that awful? can't put regular bandages on her, they simply tear her skin. she can hardly be touched . . . it just hurts too much. dehydration. age. nutrition. it's so awful to watch when she experiences pain from that. if she went to kingston, she could wind up in emergency, a lot. since her bowel and urine control is weak or gone, her briefs would have to be checked and changed frequently. i hate the thought of mom in soiled briefs for any length of time. it happens. caregivers have only so much time and so many patients. mom needs assistance for almost everything. now that i'm remembering all this, i don't see how she'll be positively evaluated. it's definitely safer at lake park. she'd either move to another section (hospice) or stay in her current room (more money.) she loves the staff. she loves her room (we made it very much her room.) as i write this, i sigh. having an aging parent, challenged with failing health, is exhausting. god bless us all who are experiencing this. it is not easy, in any regard. lake park just opened a hospice unit, which is also a plus. very very nice. kingston will break ground for a hospice unit shortly. i don't know . . . i guess it all boils down to what's best for mom, what's the safest thing, what will make mom happiest. it's a collective decision, really. mom's opinion is influenced by our thoughts. we'll see. we'll see. whatever, we have till april 24 to make a final decision, god willing. that's when mom's medicare runs out at lake park. we're getting close. i hope mom gets better and stronger so we can get to the toledo zoo, which apparently is supposed to be good. mom's tv channel of choice is animal planet. there are such great shows on that. she loves the animal shows, yet she owns a cardboard dog! i laugh. i know mom can't sit for that long but heck, we'd wheel her around that zoo so fast; i just know it would be one grand outing. i hope that happens. a goal. good to have those. a summer goal. christ, i hope the world is safe to travel in. i hope there is a miracle and there is another way. we're capable of peace. but then i think, man, humans have been fighting each other forever. maybe we're not capable. oh man. i need to go back to a university and take some world sociology courses. i'm sure we're capable of getting along. aren't we? oh man. well, those are my mixed up thoughts for today. love you, mom. hope you're having a gentle, good day mama. surprise us all. get a great evaluation from kingston. surprise me. bless you, mom. love ya to bits.

March 23, 2003

my god, another season. thank you, god. i welcome spring. we've had a horrific winter in toronto, and toledo. i remember driving a few times to toledo to see mom, thinking, jesus, i'm not driving in this again. but i did. thank god for prayer, angels, visualizing; i always had a safe trip. i pray a lot while driving. i only had one close call. it was a whiteout time. i was just, by a hair, ahead of a pileup on black ice. god almighty, i prayed, i cried. i still see it. i was a hair ahead of it all. thank you god, once again. that makes me think of "when it's your time . . ." kind of thing. i'm leaning towards that. when you're on the books, for a certain day, date, and time, i think that's it. it's pre-ordained, destined, planned. by the big kahuna. that's why i've pretty well stopped obsessing about mom's condition, her journey, her challenge. when she's called, she'll go. i'm remembering donna's e-mail from earlier today: "mom's not so good today." i hate those. it's so true; mom is not eating well or enough, not moving well or enough, and slipping, ever so slowly, again. her spirits are good. she's loving on the phone. "hi, honey girl, how are you?" of course it's always followed by "did you work today?" i laugh. oh mom. that ol' work ethic . . . it's a given. mom's saved her money; she's good with money. dad worked his butt off; mom, too. they saved. they retired, and lived well by their standards. mom has enough money to be cared for, at this time and for the next few years. christ, she did better than i did . . . and many i know. it's embarrassing! but emotionally, mom—that generation, had a mind set. work. it's not like i haven't worked; jesus, i've worked since i was sixteen. i wasn't afraid to spend the money and live; travel, experience life, take risks. i'm like three months ahead . . . that's it. i think i have enough for a funeral and all that goes with it. it's not that i'm worried, but i become more aware. mom's death is coming. we're all going to die. at one point, we go. i'm grieving for mom. already. i kind of remember there's quite the difference in these two words: grieving and mourning. grieving is the more immediate, deep shock, crying, the sorrow. mourning has to do with ongoing grief. the time, taking the time, allowing yourself to feel bleak, wear black, declare a mourning period, mourning ceremonies. i'm sure i'll get into this big time. i love my mom, so much. i'm sure you feel the same way . . . don't you? about your mom, your dad, some loved one. if not, well, there's work to be done. process. letting go. embracing. forgiving. hell, forgetting. hell, once you really start aging, you forget so much anyway! but pain is pain, and deep wounds are deep wounds. i'm thinking i'm ok. haven't felt the need for my dear therapist, dr. mary. she's good. i was doing good work on my own death and dying; the cancer and all. then it got tied up with mom's passing and issues. i'm feeling damn good. damn good. i have to say marianne williamson helps. she's like a friend. i've been reading rumi. my god, he was a gifted man. that poem, a necessary autumn inside each. it speaks to me. about living, about processing. about letting go. surrender. when i think of surrender, i also think of my other favorite poet, mary oliver and her book "new and selected poems." i believe she won a pulitzer prize for poetry for this collection. i especially like "when death comes." in fact, it's my favorite poem. then i start to think, well, hell. i've written some poems about mom. share them, charlene! so, here we go.

images

the sad, sad eyes
of some of the
sad, sad faces
of some of the
sad, sad bodies

in wheel chairs, struggling with walkers,
struggling to get in and out of whatever,
struggling to get up and down of whatever.

and the eating . . .
the struggle to get to a fork or a spoon
let alone get some food on it, then,
the long journey to one's mouth,
with the shaking . . . the shaking . . . the shaking

mom has said, with such sadness
it even hurts to lift this spoon, with tears in her eyes
her wrinkled face engulfed with tragic expression

i feel so badly for all the old people; their struggles
i can't get rid of the heaviness it has created in me
as if a personal invitation to death
was sent by each individual
with a date, and time, undecided

february 2002

mother's hands

just looking at her hands
i'd say no; no, they aren't my mom's
i'd say that because they're really disfigured
arthritis
finger joints turning in odd directions
bumps, lumps at various areas on the skin
fingers that are curled and almost crippled,
full of dark spots. very witch-like.
scary.
yet, they're fragile. have a gentle quality. look kind.

they've sewed for love.
cooked for recognition.
waited on people, for years. for love.
they wanted attention. still go wanting.
still seek love. long to be held.
but,
they are too uninviting.

winter 2001

thank you, god, for poetry and poets like mary oliver. thank you for women like my mom; lions of courage. thank you for women like me. thank you for so many things. love you, mom. thank you, god.

March 25, 2003

i'm waiting for death. for mom to die. back in her room at lake park. donna called yesterday. "mom's not so good." i was on a great work call; but had to leave on day one at 3 p.m. i would have made a shit load of money. oh well. went home, packed, went by caroline's office to say good-bye to her and the dogs (she had taken them to work), and off to toledo. arizona, too? oh god, i don't know. packed for any and all things. did emergency banking, left a message on the answering machine, and hit the road. i was driving to toledo by 6 p.m., pretty good. i was scattered, although i've been kind of prepared. in and out of tears while driving, trying to think straight. arrived in toledo at 10:30 p.m.; pretty damn fast. there was a lot of truck traffic; i had one gas fill-up and sandwich stop. no problem at the border, at all. donna had been with mother since morning. she was tired. donna has been stellar. a great caregiver and angel. after i arrive and review with donna what's up, i send her home. i stayed till 1:30 a.m. mom, i think, knows i'm here. she's pretty much out of it. it's pneumonia, some fever, no eating, hardly any liquids. she still gets the breathing treatments and an antibiotic once a day for the pneumonia. she's breathing deeply with ok intervals. she has constant care; the staff has been above and beyond in this recent decline. she's been a favorite for many; mom's no bullshit attitude and her zany, wacky sense of humor when she feels ok, aid her popularity. donna and i come back by 7:30 a.m. mom's resting comfortably. she doesn't seem to have the awful rattling sound in her lungs today. last night it sounded like she was part of an indian ceremony; so much rattling for the death angel to come. awful, awful sound. mom looked like she was dying. that look. that friggin' look. but today, no rattles. however, there are strange twitches. mom is doing a whispering thing. i watch her face and she's in a conversation with someone. something. facial reaction definitely corresponding with some energy. it's fascinating, yet spooky. i don't know if this is part of the death journey or unique to mom's journey. i had quiet time for prayer this morning. like that, need it. for mom, for me. i've my rosary, my amma beads; i'm just going at it. at one point mom wakes up in pain, with a large yelp and cry; i called for darlene. they gave her some morphine. at the same time, dear aunt barb called, mom's sister. i was half present for the call, trying to be there for mom. aunt barb can't hear all that well so even excusing myself was a bit loud and awkward. we arranged to talk later. i don't feel like talking, really. what's to say? i only want to bear witness and help mom, however i can. just think, any breath could be her last. i hate this. i'm glad i'm here. any children of dying parents . . . try, try to be there. it's an incredible experience. mom's not really conscious. she's comfortable though. this is good. respiratory just suggested a permanent mask for oxygen. the nose device isn't giving her what she needs. i called donna and she said ok. now mom has this huge mother of a mask on. she's sleeping soundly. mom's a mouth breather, so it's better. she'll get more oxygen, which she needs. she has varied body actions; ankles stretch, the odd scratching, she doesn't have the wandering death eyes, though. she's had them. not pleasant. dying is not a pretty sight. not in this case. mom's so physically challenged. in bed too long, with minimum movements, since january. the emotional challenge of someone wanting to die, pleading with god, and nothing happening, is sad to witness. i don't really know where mom is mentally, psychologically. she has always stated she's not afraid to die; "when god wants me, he'll take me." i see or sense some resistance; can't quite figure it out. it's not pleasant to wait for death. makes me think of mary oliver's poem, again. caroline has called to check up, check in. i can be so open and honest, in the moment, with her. love that woman. donna just called, heading back. i've eaten too much already today . . . damn! feeding my sorrow and sadness. i'm already in grief; starting to mourn. i don't feel well; feel unrooted once again. just getting into the swing of things at home. then, this. many things left; a new coaching client, all appointments, good call at work—nice guys, good show, good money. dogs. caroline. home. this is challenging. i don't think i'm that flexible. bit embarrassing. little things. working in the yard. postponed. feel fat. disoriented. sleep deprived. on the edge. i don't have any american money; left too fast to get some from the bank. i hate asking my sister for money, or mom. i'll take what's offered, but i hate to ask. oh well. i can talk myself into a change of attitude. get with the program, girl. it's mom. mom's death journey. nothing else matters. jesus, what i didn't throw into five bags. didn't know what to bring. and i thought i was ready. have to laugh, really. pray. god, just use me. lift me up. shake me out. kick me in the ass. nothing matters but mom. i'm having a foot problem. my one foot hurts like hell. i was actually going to get fitted for orthotics any day. had to postpone that. don't know what's up. need to walk. move. air out. i'll go out as soon as donna comes. the grounds at lake park are beautiful. i'll go commune with the birdies. jesus. i need a chiropractic adjustment, need my orthotics, need to be lighter. what i need most . . . stop the whining, girl. ah . . . donna is in the building. i'm off to chill. just too wound up. perhaps i'm afraid of death. i don't think so. but i am afraid of pain. oh god, when i'm dying, i hope i get the card that says no pain. exit fast. oh god. you know me. i am a survivor but i don't enjoy pain. you know that about me. so please, remember. please.

oh, mom. i sure hope you're going to ask the dealer for a few new cards. no more pain. no more suffering. exit fast. those would be three, mom. oh, god. please be with my mom. you two figure it out. but god, no pain for mom. please. no more. thank you. thank you, god.

March 26, 2003

mom is very clear and sharing about her funeral. no flowers! she always thought flowers were such a waste of money. donna and i agree to have some, but we tell mom, "yes, no flowers." we want her to be happy. she wants us to take the pictures off her walls (the room that she's in right now) when she dies. "yes, mom." we agree to do that. "make sure i go to church." "yes, mom." we agree to that. there are a lot of tears. previously she made me promise to "stop by the house." a drive-by. i promised. it's 3:30 in the afternoon. don't know who she is talking to but mom looks up and says, "you see what i'm saying." more tears. it' sad. i am bearing witness to mom's death. good to be here; so hard. mom whispers to "them." who the hell is she talking to? falls asleep. sleeping calmly now. this would be a good exit point for mom. is she feeling complete? she has clean briefs, clean gown. we're waiting for the angel of death. told mom how much i love her. i'll even name my future dogs after her . . . katie, kate, cath . . . we all laughed. god, i'm all over the place in my thinking. i'm remembering a dream from last night: oprah without makeup, marianne williamson, dr. wenzke, me. in an office. talking. marianne obviously pregnant. oprah offering me a job. i want to talk about marianne and who she's involved with, talk about the baby. dr. wenzke puts his hand on marianne's belly. i think oh-oh, how sweet this is, dr. wenzke and marianne. they look lovingly at each other. i'm so happy for them. i'm so excited. but oprah still wants to talk about my career and offering me something. i'm saying, "no, no. not now. let's enjoy this moment." i'm still laughing about that dream. i put a rosary in mom's hands. the assistants come in to change mom, to check on her. i say "no, don't disturb her, i think she's dying." trying to remember this great poem by rumi, about death, dying, mothers. i'll have to find it. i think i read it. i'm in a daze. mom is dying. i'm in a daze. i want to write some great poem for mom, but i can't get the words in my mind. i'm having images of white buffalo roaming around this room, around mom. it's a strange frida kahlo moment. i'm imagining a painting. i'm thinking gentle, gentle, gentle to god, jesus, mary, mother of god, all "my" angels, especially dear suzanne. be there for mom. gentle with her. gentle. mom is mouthing "i love you" to me. honestly, this is so sweet, so sad. "i love you, don't cry." somehow i am crying and saying to mom "your daughters have two very distinctly different personalities" and mom is making the cuckoo sign and smiling, looking at donna, with regards to me. "we both love you to bits, mom." we are actually having fun, the three of us, as mom is dying. this is bizarre. i'm rambling on, "how lucky you are mom, you get to go to god, go home. we get to stay and try to make it better here." everyone keeps wandering in and out, saying loving things to mom. they think she's dying too. this is intense. mom seems to be taking a lot of time to die. it seems labored. painful. i haven't thought of any poem for mom. my process is i get lines, feelings, a string of words, doesn't have to be a sentence. i am feeling one possible title, "gardenias, pizza and beer." i associate gardenias with mom; on special occasions dad would buy mom a gardenia corsage to wear. they smell so beautiful. i'm making a trade with god. i'll come back. i've always thought this was my last time around in human form; next assignment shooting star or something. but, i'll come back in exchange for no more pain for mom. no discomfort. enough of this lingering. use me again, lord.

take mom. quietly. silently. peacefully. enough. enough. enough of this agony she seems to be going through. enough, goddamn it. take me. use me. i can't stand these friggin' morphine shots. her discomfort. the curling of the hands. her yelling, sometimes crying "oh god, help me god. take me god." those pleading, sad, pained eyes of mom's. this sucks, god. if you have anything to do with this, for christ's sake, give it up. punch her time card out. let her go. for christ's sake, let her go. i look at mom; her skin is so so frail. wrinkled, dry. she's in ultra-fragile condition; heels broken down. they are red, irritated, she's developing sores. this is bad. she has the same irritations on her bum. she's been given protective sleeves for her arms, but she doesn't like them. she says it hurts more putting them on and off than they do good. her skin is sensitive to touch. she has a few tears. there is a yellowish tone to her body. i think we're into mom's final agony 9:45 a.m. another shot. groaning, coughing, and spitting up, tears. she was crying, asking again, "why am i so sick?" mary ellis, one of her superb caretakers, tries to calm mom down, saying "it's between you and god, kay. relax if you can. just relax, it's going to be ok. you just be yourself. don't put up any fronts. you feel what you feel. talk to us. we're here." goddamn, this is hard to witness. it's like a bloody war, a battle being lost. the war, too, will soon be lost. it's quiet now. mom's quiet. i feel like i'm in a nearby foxhole, watching a bloody squirmish. donna and i are in this trench with mom, but it's mom who is being shot. will die. we have to be strong. be here for the dying. that's our role. that's our responsibility. isn't it a child's responsibility? damn right it is. what next? what next? 11:19 a.m. she's still here. i was dozing a lot. donna has been holding mom's hands. mom's been mumbling. i think she's talking to "them." who the hell are "them?" then mom blurts out, "keep the eggs in the carton." other last-minute reminders. then there's a poem mom has remembered from a long time ago . . . something like "there was a little bird, that shit a little turd . . ." and on and on. we had quite the moment around 12:30 p.m. i crawled into bed with mom and cried like a little girl (acting) saying "i don't want to wear a dress to grandma's." boy, did that put a smile on mom's face. she just shook her head, like "oh yeah, you're nuts honey girl, but i love you." she's been quite emotional; crying hard. mary came in and calmed her down a bit. i didn't want mom's oxygen treatment to be intrusive. sometimes the band around the head can make mom feel irritable. so i held the mask to mom's face. she was crying, i was crying. i re-affirmed that it was ok to cry. we both were. i told her, again, how much i loved her. how proud i was of her. how courageous i thought she was. how happy i was that she was my mom. how happy i was about my life; that she should be happy because i was happy. she said she was proud of me! mom said she was proud of me! goddamn! she enjoyed hearing what i had to say, i sure enjoyed hearing what she had to say. i asked her to please be near me as an angel. she said she would always be near me. she told donna and i not to fight, be good to one another, don't fight over money. mom was crying that the girls would come in tomorrow and she wouldn't be here. i guess she meant the aides. i was crying and telling mom, "you'll never leave us, your spirit will always be with us." it was pretty complete. pretty complete. mom wore herself out. she had another shot of morphine. mary came in with a little bird pin and stuck it on mom's gown. looks like a dove. mom likes it. mary was saying something funny. it's pretty high energy in the room when mom is awake and clear; in her non-crying moments. the emotional exchanges, with whomever is here, are loving and beautiful. tender as can be; sweet. i think that's why mom is so popular. but, we're still all waiting for mom to die. it's 1:50 p.m. we've been here a long stretch. seems like days and nights. for sure, last night. slept in these uncomfortable chairs. slept? hardly. at one point i took off her "permanent" breathing mask. said we've got to put her back on "just the nose thing." that big mask was too much for her. we were called, the night before, at 3:30 a.m. i'm lost. out of it. feel like this has been some marathon telecast, but there's no end. i need to nap, need to sleep. but i don't want to miss anything, as in mom's passing. then the nurses tell you horror stories; people can last like this, for months. maybe years. oh my god.

March 28, 2003

overtired today. we gave serious consideration to stay overnight again, but the staff said no. go home. brother, we were so tired, we listened. today, she's sweet, somewhat alert. kind of babyish in her talking. said she was going on her trip today, "i'm going straight to heaven." she's being very funny and friendly. it's bizarre. she's propped up now for better breathing. the nose apparatus is working fine. all seems to be ok, at the moment. last time mom's oxygen level was checked it was in the mid 90's. her vitals; all good. just haven't a clue what's going to happen today. honestly, i'm so surprised she's alive. mom said she is feeling better and whatever she's had, it passed. i just laugh; there's nothing else to do. whatever, it's passed. she really hasn't had much to eat for a few weeks. gandhi, move over. this is a woman who can handle no food. when you think of it, very little food or liquids, minimal comfort care, meaning no pills, no medicine, only morphine when she's in pain, which she is in constantly; i don't get it. we've had closure, we've had instructions, we've had suggestions, made the funeral plans, tears, lots of prayers. the whole bit. she's at peace. we're at peace. we're all just waiting for death. this sucks. that's what's up; we're waiting for death. around noon, mom says, "i'm going soon." continues with something like, "going, going, gone. it's going to be fast." she has her rosary and a picture of blessed mary from rome, she says dad is here. she starts crying heavily and uncontrollably.

some staff come in, we are all crying. mom continues to say she is going, going straight to heaven. she looks around and sees us crying. she says, "i want to go out laughing. i don't want you all to cry," which makes us do that cry/laughing thing. it was such a moment. donna had gone to the hairdresser; i called ron and said, "get donna here, now." mom and i had closure again, saying we loved each other. i asked mom to be my special angel. she said she'd always be with me. donna and ron come running in. i had taken mom's breathing thing off. i mean, she was going. mom gave donna and i a few reminders about not fighting, the funeral. it was all sad. then mom was talking with god, "ok, i'm ready." we all got quiet and watched, waited. donna and i holding hands with mom. after a bit of time, donna called the nurse, as mom was still breathing, now complaining about pain. nothing else happened. mom didn't pass. mom got another shot, everyone recovered from the announced passing and no passing, and we all slowly got into supporting mother, again. when she woke up, there was another "serial personality" (my own term: she did seem to have a few going on). this time a young, innocent, sweet, funny girl. a complete turnaround. i was totally shocked. totally. i was befuddled. donna sent me on errands, although i had nothing to do. i think i was freaking out, silently. it's so draining to go through these episodes. you're happy, you're sad, confused, angry. i went and did nothing. the doctor came. he's confused, too. are we back to square one? another rebuild? another resurrection? my friend laurie calls mom "the queen of resurrections." i use that term all the time now, for that's what she is. i can't imagine what mom feels like, but then, maybe she's lost it mentally. she goes in and out of these personalities, near-death experiences, in and out of what seems horrific pain, and in and out of being somewhat normal. i'm back in the room, exhausted, as are donna and ron. they're going. i'll stay till early evening; make sure she's ok. as it happens, i tried to leave at 8 p.m. but mom started a crying anxiety attack, cries of spine pain, pain in her butt, itching sensations. lots of tears. cries for help. screaming, "help me, help me." more morphine. she settled down. lakesha, a great aide, and i sat with her. i was too worn out to stay any longer. i felt sleep deprived. when i get in that state i'm short on patience. i can be/am a bitch. i hate my impatience. but that's a part of me. i finally left. got to donna and ron's; donna is already sound asleep. i went right to bed. totally exhausted in every way. the next day, we were both up, dressed, and out of the house by 7:30 a.m. just worried about mom. we get there and mom's ok. mary was in talking to her; donna and i changed her. the doctor came in. we're all baffled that she's alive. "we'll try to stay on top of the anxiety attacks; that'll still be comfort care. it's good you're both here." something like that from dr. wenzke. i've cried all morning. i'm mad as hell at god. mom's ready. we've had closure, she has no real quality going on, on any level. why is she still here? i'm crying all the time. i want morphine. mom is starting to say to me; "you always look at me like i'm dying." she wants me to change my look. so i've apologized. explained some of the experiences. i've agreed to try and change my look. now i'm pissed off at mom too. pretty dismal, eh? hell, i'm pissed at donna too. why not? i'm just pissed. i want this to be over! i'm ashamed. but i'm honest. i'm honest. oh, i'd better listen to my marianne tapes and pray. this is bad. this is my dark side; phew. i don't like it. don't like it. this moment is a bad living dream. i'd better breathe. really breathe. i'd better get a grip. i'm not in the now. when in the now, i love mom. donna. life. it's just challenging; sad. i think i'm torn about leaving. should i leave? is this going to go on for weeks, months? god forbid, years? should i worry about money? i feel guilty because i even have those thoughts. i can't leave donna here, alone with this, in this. i've got to calm down. think logically. fight my way back to now. to calm. to peace. i'll go for a walk. i'll breathe. i'll go sit in the church. i'll listen to marianne. no . . . i'm going to talk with god. start off angry and shouting; then, wait. maybe i'll hear him/her/it. i don't think it matters what we call that god energy. it may not have a form, folks. it may be just the biggest, best thought we can ever muster up. whatever. i'm going to go connect with that. i need to. i can't stand me right now. i can't. god, help me. please help me. i'll listen. i will. help me, please. god, help me.

March 29, 2003

here with mom. arrived at 9 a.m.; donna here at 7:30 a.m. they put mom on the commode today for a poop; that really wore her out. why did they do that? i guess she's really wanting to go for it, in her final days. it's so degrading to poop in her diaper. think about it. not even your friggin' pants. she's tired. she is trying. god bless her. she's at her wits end; if mom could will herself to die, i'm sure she would. she's a bit complicated at the moment; has this little girl thing happening. a little girl voice and actions. serial personality? who knows? she's this little girl; polite, cute. then there's this woman in pain, body breaking down, sores on her butt, skin breaking down, sensitive everywhere. tears earlier because it hurts when you touch her. skin tears easily. that's a big problem. she's been in bed so long it's like a living coffin. hard for her to get comfortable because her little butt just can't handle it anymore. no matter what position they place her in. her oxygen is 87 today. low again. i sure hope we don't do the mask; i hate it. covers up so much of her face. she pooped again, only this time on the bedpan. she drank a little water. there's a constant cry of pain when in a waking state. i've cried all morning. i need relief; maybe a movie. what's mom dying of? is she dying? god forbid the reality for mom, if some stories i hear are true. people can linger months, years . . . god forbid, not like this. not like this. for sure mom will stay at lake park. maybe go down to hospice care; april 24 is the decision-making date. i'll stay until friday and go home. it's a difficult decision. i have a money-making opportunity next saturday, a day to recover, and then i have to call for work and make some money. i've lost two weeks of work. i'm so broke. get out of my ego shit. rise up, girl. it'll all come out in the wash, as they say. concentrate on being in the moment. mom is dying and i bitch about money in my head. got to do some spiritual reading. get in a different mind set. i'm reading so many books at the moment; one by marianne williamson, one by naomi levy. very helpful. i feel better. praying does help. such a process. a friggin' process. i had two good phone calls last night. soothing, spiritual. my friends try to make me laugh. that's good for me. my anger with this process could be a dark and funny comedy act. today, caroline called from "the land." she's always a comfort; a soothing soul. my rock. i feel badly for mom. so badly. i hope her time is up soon. i'll trust god, once again. such a mystery. i realize god doesn't cause the suffering. i guess all mom's life's decisions up to this point got her here; smoking for one, nutrition and diet another, being physically inactive. negative attitude came later. grew as time went on; health failed. i sometimes question her honesty about a spiritual life and connection. i don't know if she is even praying now. i see no signs of it. that doesn't mean it isn't happening. it's a mystery. once we pass, i guess we'll know the real story. what happens to soul? where does that energy really go? i asked marianne about that once. i think she told me we don't go anywhere. i must continue that conversation because it puzzles me. perhaps one gift of the human form is we try to figure out things. gift? duh. all i continue to learn is 1) we're not in charge and 2) the more i get into detaching, the better my life goes. i try to focus on my heart, mind, body, soul. constantly remember i am a child of god, here to live and give the light. that's my mission. sounds easy. not. but good to be clear. i'm at my best when i pray in the morning, connect with god, move my body as in walking, set my goals and intentions for the day. holding hands with god through the day works for me. i must say there is a plethora of spiritual material out there. my god if you, the reader, can't find something to resonate with, mama mia, you must be dead. so much out there. take the time to read and find your path. it's our purpose to do that. then live it. but that's my take. thank god for marianne. i'm kind of embarrassed; i almost feel like she's an invisible friend. i do talk to her at church, fax or write her when appropriate. not that invisible. i imagine we'd be good friends. same vibrational field. i don't have that many friends who are so spiritual. my friends are good people, fine people. however, not as deeply into the spiritual journey, meaning, and exploration of it all. guylaine, she's one. and a beautiful one. maybe you have to almost die; then you get it. who knows? for christians or is it just catholics who say this, christ will come again. i do feel that's about our own awakening. it's when we all awaken to that highest magnificence within us. wake up. we, you, me; we are being called! i'm trying to remember what marianne said in church last sunday. something regarding "we rise above the battlefield." we are capable of rising above the battlefield. within the context of her talk, it was brilliant. i'll have to look at my notes. i do believe god is rooting for us. rooting for all of us to discover the love in our hearts, for everyone, everything. then we can create the systems for people to get along. it's not rocket science. i think we, all of us, hold onto "well, we've/they've fought for centuries. it can't change." well, i'm sorry. just because it's always happened a certain way, is no reason to hold onto something. i look at mom and pray she'll be an important angel. maybe mom can help with peace, from the other side. mom, i'll help you on this side. let's work together! tell me, show me, talk to me, when you go. i'll help, you know i will. i'm going to hold mom's hand for a while. stop writing. pray for god to be here. for god to talk to or maybe take this big angel. well, she's kind of little. but she's big. you know what i mean. god bless us all. god help us all. god, let us all find the way, the key to help ourselves. help us find the way to be as big as we can. for ourselves. for each other. and so it is. god bless.

March 30, 2003

another brilliant marianne williamson day at renaissance unity in warren, michigan. i had to go. marianne is there, periodically. mom's pretty zonked today; donna in the room early. i called from warren to see if i could stay for the second service. it was fine. mom's "just resting." i felt guilty staying for the second service, but i need the strength i get from god via marianne. i'm riding high; even though i cried all the way back from warren. i arrived in mom's room; donna and nance were there. then they took off. i'll go for a walk later; i'm good, tank full. mom's out of it. god bless her. she's only had morphine this morning. mmm. i think she's failing. much weaker. i've decided to stay for a few days? longer? is she dying? will she linger? it's so hard to know what to do. i mean there are a lot of stories about how this can go on and on. i'll have a long talk with god. turn it over. i so want to be with mom when she passes; i just don't want her to be alone. no one should be alone. now i get the mother teresa thing. i always wanted to go to calcutta. work with her; for her. for them. the forgotten. the dying. oh jesus. sweet jesus. be with mom, please. will i ever work again? will i be eating cat food when i'm old? i go there in an instant. how stupid. i've lost so much money. it's all about the money in this life, isn't it? oh god. forgive me. no, mom, forgive me. i'll stay. however long it takes, i'll stay. and god willing, i'll be with you when you die. i've got such happy thoughts. i reunited with a woman from church, "andy." it was nice. such a beautiful soul. her eyes are filled with unconditional love. some pain and sorrow, too. she had moved to new york. she's back. good to see her. do i know her? no. are we connected? yes. i feel that way with marianne too, but she has hundreds, if not thousands, that feel that way. i honestly feel connected to both. andy has a healing presence around her. i like that. also saw marcie, another slave of marianne's. just joking. it takes a village to help marianne. i feel at home at the church. man oh man. marianne was powerful today. phew. she's either channeling or an angel or has such a high vibration. i can't imagine her "offstage." well, i can. she's no different. that's what's unique about her. she just is. i can always apply what marianne talks about to my life, right then and there. immediacy. god bless marianne. you know we've experienced mom's passing, well, a few times. closure, tears, requests, all things said. and then, no death. tears my heart out. i'm angry with god. she wants to go. ready. willing. and she doesn't leave. why? why? why? i don't get it. i don't. it's authentic: the good-byes, sobs, truth, touching, holding hands. snot dripping from nose. the ugliness. the beauty. the tenderness. and then, no exit. after the non-dying, i am begging, praying, to be here, be here fully. accept the rehearsals. don't miss the play! mom is disappointed she's still alive. i have no answers. i encourage her to keep praying. i found myself rude, short-tempered, mean when mom requested something, a while back. i can't even remember. i was cranky. then she started to cry, about the pain, about being alive. oh, i felt bad. ashamed. god give me strength. i'm renewed after church, after marianne. and again i ask, god . . . hello . . . who's in charge? please, hear my mom. really hear her. let her know what she has to do. you know her. talk to her. please. mom is suffering. i don't think that's acceptable. we've pills, procedures, and we've god. one of the three, take her down. take her. my mom should not be suffering. simple as that! i don't think i'll ever get the full understanding of this situation till i pass. ask about this. mom has these little tears coming out of the side of her eyes. then she mumbles. and talks. god only knows. maybe it's the negotiation. carry on, mom. i'm tired. did not sleep well again last night. had a lousy dream about jealousy. possession and jealousy. not my good suits in this life. ok now, after years of therapy. but embarrassed by my behavior with these qualities, earlier on. i didn't sleep at all after 1:30 a.m. tossed and turned, prayed. got up at 6 a.m. and left for church. oh my god. mom just cried out because her heels hurt her so badly. her body is breaking down because of being in bed. more frequent "god, help me" cries. i just asked for morphine. if i had my way, i'd overdose her. would god punish me? i don't think so. i can't believe we are to witness such suffering and do nothing. i can't believe it. she wakes up and cries, "why am i so sick? help me, what's the matter with me?" i don't think mom is here mentally. but i don't know. she's really going down a road. there's a palsy kind of thing happening with her right arm and hand. trembling. to me, her stomach seems so damn large. bloated. my god, this is pretty ugly. thank god the staff is good with mom. all their patients. this hacking and spitting. emphysema. damn ugly. don't smoke. don't smoke. don't smoke. this is ugly. such a terrible way to die. thank god mom doesn't smell. the room doesn't smell. i hate that urine smell. mom's always powdered up. she smells good. mom gets powdered in her vaginal area, and i said to mom, "there are not a lot of women with elizabeth taylor between their legs." (that's the powder we use) well, aide mary and i just started to laugh and laugh. good comic relief, for an instant. mom wasn't awake enough to enjoy the remark. and if elizabeth taylor ever reads this, really, it was only a joke in the moment. it gave us much needed relief. thank you. donna just called; she's tired. i said stay home. i'm good. she's wearing out. we all are. we're going to have to have a lot of energy for arizona, when mom passes. i have to review this morning in church. remember the strength i felt. it's like i never left the room.

we've had a horrible moment in the last little while. some goddamn nurse came in and gave mom a shot of morphine in her arm, not in the "butterfly," where it's supposed to go. wrong place. she hurt mom. goddamn it. she hurt mom. i want to kill her! i raised hell. i call for the supervisor. mom is crying. i'm crying. the stupid nurse hadn't a clue. someone new. oh god, it was a horrible mistake. goddamn it. we calmed mother down with cold cloths on her forehead, telling her how sorry we were. mom was yelling at the nurse. the nurse thought the butterfly thing looked like an i.v. how does this happen? i'm even in the damn room! mom's calm now. she didn't need this. i am writing this up. reporting it. i'm so damn angry. mom has a new bruise. her arm is so tender and tattered. mom's had some extra pills. everyone hovering, being nice. i'm still so angry, i could really take a swing at someone. something. honestly, that happened with me in the room. if ever i had a lot of money, i'd institute/mandate a "big brother" watch of some kind. people to watch people. this was an accident. but my mom just doesn't need an accident right now. i can't handle another thought. i gotta go, get the hell out of here. oh mom, i'm so sorry. so sorry. so sorry. i hope you're feeling ok. how could you, though? i feel so terrible. responsible. it just happened so fast. i just didn't watch the nurse. so sorry, mom. i'm so embarrassed. damn. i feel i let my mom down. damn. everyone's on alert, mom. everyone's going to be very, very careful. oh, mom. so sorry. god, please be here. please make my mom feel either ok or take her. damn it. come on god, be here.

March 31, 2003

a day of raw emotion. mom's bad. many tears. we think it's close. mom's left hand is swollen. difficult to look at. donna took mom's ring off; i'm wearing it. i've explained to mom why; don't want her to think there is a "zorba the greek" thing going on. remember that movie, the horrible scene where people took things from the dying woman's house and she hadn't passed yet? mom is bad. i've been crying pretty much all day; i've talked with the nurse to find out what's up. donna is good about telling me it's close, but then i like to hear it from another source. i guess i can't believe it. in one breath, it could end. poor mom, so miserable. woke up crying in pain. she's not able to lift her right arm to scratch her head. the priest was in. i always leave messages at the front desk; get the priest here! one priest; so many beds, wards, hospitals. mom doesn't seem that concerned for communion or a priest. i think she's too out of it. oh god, when i die, i'm calling for everything, everyone. i'd want marianne there. hope i know her by then. i always imagined i'd take my life; in a king-size bed, filled with friends, donna, caroline, the dogs, barney . . . many others in the room. we'd drink champagne, laugh, tell stories. i'd take a pill. surrounded by love; quietly close my eyes, have a hand on each dog, barney on my chest, fall asleep. the big sleep. i now know death can be friggin' ugly. harsh, cruel, painful, sad. perhaps we should plan our departures. seems like an intelligent thing to do, really. i know, is it our right? oh jesus, i hope i get to chat with someone from the other side about this; get input. the way mom is leaving sucks. the priest is here. thank god. we pray. he prayed the sacrament of the sick and dying. don't know the official catholic name. that catholic faith; i must talk to the pope. it's fucked. i'm sorry. anti-gay, anti-abortion, anti-birth control . . . anti . . . anti love. and hello; how about the priests and little boys? duh? and any punishment of any kind going on? duh? i don't get it. i'm sure god doesn't get it. mom's crying again. her legs hurt. she fell asleep. she wakes, she cries. she falls asleep, again. so sad. one of the "mary's" just helped me change mom's position; everything hurts, every position hurts. sorry, mom. tempted to help mom; do the pillow over the face. i know i couldn't, but god, i just want to help my mom. you get jaded . . . but you witness, you pray, you cry, you beg god, you do . . . help her. take her. i wonder where the hell is he? the nurse just popped in asking "any pain?" they pop in, she's sleeping. they're not around, she wakes, she cries out, she moans. she shouldn't be alive, really. donna's started to empty mom's "closet." little bits of clothing; she'll never wear any of it. everyone says, "anytime now." jesus, no one knows. mom's pulse is dropping. mom. what can we do? you're surrounded by love. mom, you are. i'm praying the rosary pretty regularly. a catholic at heart? no. duh. i love beads! oh mom, rise above the battlefield. rise above. now mom's bum is breaking down. sores. what else can go wrong? she has no choice but to be on one side or the other. painful for her. whatever her position, she looks uncomfortable. this is so ugly. i can't stand it. it's 1:40 p.m. mary and i changed mom; moaning and groaning. i never want mom in a soiled diaper, if i can help it. come on, god. if it's not her time, please take her early. i'm appealing; re-assessment for catherine roycht. truly, i am. take some time from me. off my life. give me mom's suffering. take my mom. take my mom. i'm praying. i'm crying. i'm pleading with you, god. come on. take my mom.

April 1, 2003

last night, between 6 and 7:30, mom had an awful time. we gave her morphine at 6, but it didn't help. she was crying hard, groaning "oh god, help me. oh god, i hurt, hurt." it was bloody awful. i was crying the whole time mom was. it's agonizing to watch mom suffer. finally, they gave her more morphine at 7:30. she finally calmed down. she was out of it. i left shortly after; i was drained. once i hit my crying stage, i am simply no good. mother is surrounded by help; they continually urge the family to take breaks, go home. i just wanted to be in bed with a scotch and cry; watch mind-numbing tv. thank god for "boston public," one of my favorite shows. enjoy that jerri ryan. hot. i really do love that show; hell, i'd teach there! it helped me calm down. i'm so tired. my body aches. not feeling well; drained. that awful drain from waiting for death. watching mom suffer. we're all affected. i try to hang in "my" room when here; christ, i've been here so long. donna and ron need their time, a sense of home and each other. damn i miss home and my life. but honestly, i wouldn't miss this; it's where i'm supposed to be. makes you find out what you're made of! keep learning more about compassion, patience, gratitude. i'm still in a very animated conversation with god about what it is all about. praying constantly to just let go. god's time, not mine. people suffer. loved ones suffer. not easy. pray and bear witness. that's all i can do, and be as loving as possible. daily morning mass helps when i make it, which is often. i try to say a rosary a day for mom. that helps. well, i mark a calendar year tomorrow. no big deal. i plan to have a big sixty-fifth, next year. survived cancer of the colon. became more spiritual. want to celebrate love: for myself, my soul, my friends, my family. i tell everyone i'm marrying myself on my sixty-fifth. truth is, i married myself long ago. during the cancer. in my heart. but i'd like to celebrate that love. mom won't be here for that, that's for sure. i'll wear her ring. that'll be "the love" ring. that's nice. mom's in and out of consciousness. she can't linger much longer. her skin breaking down so badly. heels, especially. she also complains about her spine, back, toes, legs. poor thing. a body can only take so much. sometimes i get a feeling . . . like some communion with god . . . a peaceful feeling in the midst of all this shit . . . that it's ok. it's going to be ok. a wave of peace or love just passes through. maybe that's pure love. it comes more so with slow breathing, no agenda. when i don't try to push the river. i guess it's "the now." a pretty powerful feeling, the now. have you read eckart tolle's "the power of now?" good read. sometimes i get up and have to look closely at mom; see if she's alive. although normally i hear the deep, challenged breathing, sometimes there's a quietness. very spooky. there are these pauses; they become more pronounced . . . longer . . . and i think, my god, is this the end? then, a very deep breath. i wish mom could be above her own battlefield. i have mom's ring on the second day in a row. i'm not a jewelry gal. an amma bracelet. i have one silver ring from the navajos in arizona. that's it. but i'm wearing mom's ring. i like it. my two ma's; amma and mom. marianne's my angel. i've good women in my spiritual life. lucky. i have a dull ache in my head today. a heaviness. not eating well at all. trying to have no more than two drinks a night. not enough walking. you'd think it would be easy to stay on top of life, through this challenge, nutritionally. my efforts have just collapsed. it's the energy level. drained. then no energy for any good decisions. it's like you just survive. not much more. i need a massage, that's really one thing i do need. i'm crying enough, so i feel i'm releasing my sadness. i'm being pretty honest with my feelings; even about the money. i talked with donna this morning. she'll be giving me some. that's good. what a trip: mom's dying, friggin' war in iraq, nothing to get up about. but then, i visualize god with me, marianne or amma, and i behave in a better manner. hold higher thoughts. i've grabbed a new book, "new revelations/conversations with god" by neale donald walsch. it's pretty good. has some powerful suggestions. i can't believe how the concept of god turns off so many people. maybe disappointed when they were young, by god? never really exposed to god? a crying shame that parents don't introduce children to many ideologies. then let kids discuss and choose their path. they've got to have the information to choose whatever, even if it's nothing. those of us who do believe, vocalize. christ almighty. vocalize. we must all consciously act with love, live with love. which is god, is it not? i love when marianne says "rehearsal is over! it's time to act our best. do our best." she's funny without trying to be. for me, acting with love, being love as much as i can, that's the mission. my mission. to be here for mom. in the moment of passing. to love to the very end; as honestly and as authentically as i can. i will. i will do that. i just get tired. which i am now. i think i just talked myself into being in the now. in love. with god. here. with mom. so this is good. enough writing for today. i want to be with my mother. watch her. tend to any need. pray for her. love her. love her with my eyes, my heart, my mind. with as much full attention as i'm capable of.

April 2, 2003

my sixty-third birthday. i celebrated with morning mass, doing a bit of research at barnes and noble on diaries, journals, etc.; and faxing my supportive letter to congressman dennis kucinich about his proposed department of peace legislation. what a good thought, action. my god, why aren't we all behind that, 1,000%? i actually met him at a global renaissance alliance peace conference in warren, michigan; hosted at the great renaissance unity. facilitated by the great marianne williamson. he is croatian, i think. he's some part of the former yugoslavia, for sure. he is an absolutely brilliant man, great thinker, good politician. that conference should have been a prime time tv special. things everyone should know about things like this and the people involved. he spoke humanely, thoughtfully, and intelligently about how we, it, can be. he'd be a good president! marianne, a good first lady! have no idea if they date. surely, they are good friends. i've actually changed my behavior since that conference. always have reminders to pray for peace on my answering machine, send good thoughts out to the universe, constantly. pray more. for a better way. we can do it, we humans. we can. there are many organizations working for peace; get on the internet. definitely support the g.r.a., what a good group they are; founded or co-founded by marianne. my god, they are active. that's it, isn't it? we have to be active to change anything . . . ourselves, our community, our government, our world. so, get active! we're too self-absorbed. sinful. take an inventory. are you sinful? i've had a good birthday morning. back in mom's room. it's a beautiful day. she's about the same. we're being a bit more proactive with the morphine, since she hurts so badly. whatever is allowed, we're on it. to the tee. she's resting comfortably. she's wished me a happy birthday; no doubt prompted by my big sistah. a couple of times. nice smile, too. that's a great present. i don't think she'll die today. somehow i just don't think she will. but, god's call, god's deed. whatever. i'm ok if she goes on my birthday. i'm reading spiritual literature and donna suggested i read it out loud. so i did. some martin luther king stuff. wow, powerful. i wished i had marched with the mr. king, jr. damn. oh well, i was in the peace corps. a kennedy gal. did something. i should have gone south upon returning home. oh, well. do my bit, today. start again, today. do something, today. very odd; i read a passage about impatience. man, that hits home. "but the people grew impatient on the way; they spoke against god and against moses." numbers 21: 4-5. my mantra today, "god, give me patience. help me accept your way, not mine. your time, not mine." i lose my patience in the flick of an eye or whatever that saying is. i do. i hate mom's suffering. hate missing my life. impatience. selfishness. a normal human being? no. can't accept that. we're, i'm, better than this! i find that awareness of my breathing helps with my impatience. i need to breathe. i know saying any beads, the rosary or amma's beads, is very good for me. i find waiting for death such a hard thing. it seems close. it's a mystery. mom's mumbling more. i wonder if she's talking to dad? i'm not that happy with the catholic church; haven't heard a good thing that i can relate to this week at mass. marianne is much better to listen to. guess it's just my time with her messages. i find that the catholic church is negative. at least compared to unity, marianne, a course in miracles, unitarian, religious science, m.c.c. of toronto. any of those; that's positive. they feature a loving, supportive god. i feel connected to god. i don't like him at times; sometimes i'm so friggin' angry with him. but i know he knows me; thinks i'm an ok gal. in fact, i feel he likes a questioning soul. he likes when someone is alive, especially when we're supposed to be alive. i'm good with my god, my connection, my love/hate relationship, which is really love. i just don't understand some stuff; want more information. it's twenty past noon. i'll keep reading out aloud, what the heck. donna and ron will be coming shortly. i may go for a walk in this marvelous park system here, in toledo. i really like this city; it's so green. the park system is truly great. it's a majorly gorgeous day out. if mom doesn't die in the next few days, i'll have to consider going home. i wish i knew what to do. i'll have to meditate for guidance on this, again. this makes me think of when donna and i were doing a few overnights with mom, here. so overtired. i think donna said at one point, "if mom's not dead by 9, i'm leaving." i laughed so hard at that. it's the title of this diary because it represents how bloody tiring this dying process can be. how callous we can become. i really don't have the luxury of an open-ended schedule; need to work. i'll have to negotiate with donna for some money. i thought we'd be in arizona and back by now. away from home almost a month. can't even think in terms of lost wages. mom's dying. i'm here. end of story. if she lingers . . . will she? . . . i need to know god. i need to know. it's a miracle she's lasted this long. comfort care. she should have been long gone. must be processing. god bless mom. it's between you and god, mom. god, it's between my mom and you. love you mom. thank you for bringing me into the world, giving me birth, loving me, giving me so so much. you have been such a great mom. truly, you have. i have so many memories floating through my mind and heart at this moment. i'm going to just sit with them. savor them. thank you mother. i love you. i do. thanks.

April 3, 2003

mom seems to be a bit more peaceful today. it was sad yesterday; a lot of pain, her hands were so swollen. looked like animal hands. gator-like. ugly. awful to look at. generally a day of non-movement on my part; a draining day. i sure thought mom would pass. i came as soon as i got up. donna was too beat to come in early. as luck would have it (i'm questioning the meaning of sayings, but this one seems to make sense to me) donna and ron got a call from mike in turkey. isn't that great? the turks kept them pretty immobile there; his unit will most likely return home (germany.) slight possibility of iraq; depends on the situation. donna, ron, and i went to the elks for salad, burgers, and beer; then donna and i returned to mom's room. donna was sure she was going to go soon. but mom didn't. mom just called for a pain pill. she has been pretty talkative till now; channeling that sweet, young, naive personality. i still swear when she's mumbling, she's talking to the other side. mom's acknowledged donna this morning; hasn't really seen me yet. i started the rosary; at one point mom looked over and said, "i'm going to sleep now." i put her rosary in her hands, not knowing what she meant. then she started to do this grabbing thing with her hands. grabbing into thin air. donna told me that some people do that when they are about to die. the doctor was in this morning; mom didn't acknowledge his presence. i asked him if people in this stage (like mom is) linger too much longer; he said no. i don't know why i ask him things like that. guess i'd like to know, control, be in charge. yet, it's none of my friggin' business, is it? really. between god and mom. i'm here. till it happens. i have to grow so much more. mom seems to be at peace. that's good. she has had some sweet smiles in her sleep. mom just said, "i can hear your voice and see your face, daddy. and everyone's around me." that's as nurse darlene gave her another shot of morphine. she's actually getting very low amounts. truly, pain management. now she mumbled she thought my aunt pauline would be there. aunt pauline has alzheimer's and is in a facility in barrington, illinois. that's pretty weird. mom continues to talk. "charlene will have to drive me home. i can't see you anymore daddy." oh my god. she's still mumbling. now, she's nodded off. oh my. mary, one of her favorites, came in to check on her. i think we all think it could be anytime. mary asked, "how are you doing?" it was so damn cute. mom heard the question. she paused, and then said, as if she was a great profound thinker, "well . . ." then mary called in the other mary. we call her "indian mary" as she has a long dark ponytail. she's funny and always does this bowing thing to mom. as if mom's royalty. mom enjoys it. mom is looking like a native indian. her face, her hair. what a beautiful person. handsome. no doubt, in a past life—native indian. her hands now each hold a rolled up washcloth; to protect her from scratching and digging into her own skin. she has long nails. painted red, i might add. mom always enjoyed well manicured and polished nails. she closes her fists tightly; so this is a good safety precaution. i see less swelling in her hands and arm today, but those are my "loving eyes." i see differently each day, depending on my mood. i haven't walked or stretched in a few days; feeling bloated, heavy. dying is draining. what a heavy immobile energy it presents. donna just said, "mom's opened her eyes several times and smiled. might want to put that in your diary." i occasionally look up, thinking it's near. at one point i was just standing, staring out the window. mom wanted to know what i saw. i shared about the rainy day, as best i could. throughout this journey, i do question, wonder about mom's willingness to let go. does she have a fear of dying? is god really in charge of the plan? indeed i question "the time to die" theory; is it encoded in us? birth and death part of a master plan? do we have a say in the time, manner of our entry or exit? i'm wondering about mom's depression through the years. we suspect this was a big problem. her doctor in sun city, dr. mehta, for years said mom was depressed. encouraged her to go live with donna (donna always offered that option to mom). mom would have no part of that suggestion, or take any medication. if she was depressed, clinically depressed, and was treated with proper medication, would she be any different now? would dying be easier? would letting go be easier? less fear, if there is fear? i wonder. she's now mumbling about "i can't get up" and that's true. she's pretty low on energy and strength. she's very upset about that. donna just calmed her down. "mom, you don't have to get up for anything. you're fine. charlene and i are here. you're fine." i can't imagine wanting to move, wanting any and all that was formerly yours, and not being able to access it. i'm sad for mom. i took a break for an hour or so. drove around, listening to a marianne williamson c.d. on self love, self image. how high they are will determine your opportunity to be the best you can be. i don't think mom had a real high self image. or a lot of self love. not really. i think it's a bit of a generational thing; mom's background and experiences. i know i'll be pretty brave regarding my death; with my understandings, beliefs, experiences. when i had cancer of the colon, and that friggin' bag, i know there were times when i completely had zip. zip about anything. and a fear of death. thank god for therapy. if the circumstances were different, i'd be with marianne, congressman kucinich, and other global renaissance alliance folk, in washington. these next few days they'll be working on the department of peace proposal effort. may god be with them all and the bill.

especially the bill. for some reason i am remembering eleanor roosevelt. am i dreaming or did she come to our peace corps training in new paltz, new york? that would be summer of '62. i think she came. i sat at her feet. at any rate, i've always loved and admired the woman. use a lot of her quotes. one of my favorites is "it isn't enough to talk about peace. one must believe in it. and it isn't enough to believe in it. one must work for it." i have a great picture of her. did some reading on her. watch most documentaries on her. what a woman. god bless all who are working for peace! came back into the room, mom is crying about her ankles; "my ankles hurt me, oh god, both ankles. oh god, help me." this is so friggin' sad. oh mom. if i could take your pain away, i would. god, please, be here, now. help my mom. please.

April 4, 2003

donna and i are watching the american movie channel. "how green was my valley" is one of my all-time favorites. i remember watching it when i was a child. either the family saw it at the alamo on kedzie avenue, or was it chicago avenue? we used to go to the movies (i think) monday nights. get there before six and watch a double feature. we were young. now that i think of it, wow. that was something. no wonder i'm a movie addict. i don't remember mom or dad enjoying movies as they got older. i think i also saw this movie on our big magnavox tv . . . a huge mother of a console. we lived at 730 n. spaulding. this huge tv was in our living room. i'm sure dad bought it as soon as it was made. i somehow associate this movie with my family. now mom's yelling about her toes; total pain. "oh god, help me. i'm going to die." donna is stroking mom's head, "it's ok to go mom. it's ok to go." donna's washing her face and putting some lotion on. "let go, mom. no more pain. dad's there. we're here. let go, mom. no more pain." mom's yelling more now. god, please hear her. take her. please. it's 10:50 a.m. this last hour has been difficult. the doctor came and ordered more morphine because of the breakdown in her feet, plus mom's been crying a lot. so much discomfort; just miserable. she's restless, verbal. her bones ache, she's got pain everywhere. donna and mary changed her position, her brief, she cried. mom keeps waking up, yelling, crying in pain, then falls back to sleep for a few moments.

she looks whiter to me, this is eerie. is there no end? it's 1:55 p.m. i feel in a daze. donna went off on an errand. i'm feeling badly for mom. mary peeked her head in; to see if she could do anything. donna called; doing a few more things. mom's moaning and groaning. thoughts just come and go; in no kind of pattern. nothing is making sense. what's mom searching for? a person? god? what connection is missing? do you let go? does the force take you? is it pre-determined? i have no friggin' answers. i'm numb. i'm a witness to a lousy death. this isn't the picture i had in mind. i'm so sorry for you, mom. you don't, you really don't, deserve this suffering.

April 5, 2003

a long cry with caroline this morning. that always helps me. back in the room; mom's now yelling, "i have two bodies. take this blanket off me!" then a constant moaning and groaning. she had morphine, orally, at 6 or 6:30, had a shot at 8:30; she can have that every hour. donna thinks (and it's just thinking) maybe we change the medicine. my immediate reaction, because i'm tired, stressed, and feeling trapped in this death process is, how? why? why do anything now? i don't think when overtired. i react, usually negatively. i'm ashamed of myself. we discuss the idea, with some intelligence. what can we do? we just want to help. that's it. it's seems hopeless; we're helpless. i'm overeating; i eat whatever is on mom's trays. eat it all. emotionally empty and filling. this is not good. this frontline of dying, near death, it's bloody hard. caroline calmed me down today; she's my rock. i'm going to pray now, then continue. phew . . . i feel better. able to be here more fully. the blackness, the ugliness, selfishness, self-pity; comes and goes. i guess that's human. you admit it, deal with it. get on with it. this is your exit mom; damned if i'm not going to be as present as i can be, with and for you. mama, i love you so much. god, it's only 9:50 a.m. feels like i've lived through a twenty-four hour period, already. mom's looking at me; " i didn't know who you were . . . now i do. i'm a bit better today." that was weird. she's out of it. glad for those words. i stroke her head. she's spitting up orange juice. 10:30 a.m. another oral dose of morphine. mom's rambling. "this is not a good world. i can't breathe. i'm going away. i can't see. i can't breathe." she's dying again. donna comes. mom says, "too late." mom's saying to us, "you go." i'm smiling and telling mom, "you go, mom. you're older. you're in more pain than me. you go, mom." it's noon; she's still here. she gets another shot in the butterfly at 1:15 p.m. for pain. continually saying, "i'm in pain." i'm replying "i know mom." her reply, "no, no you don't know. don't say that!" around two mom says she can't breathe, she's going to die. i calm her down. donna and ron come back. i can't handle it. i have to go for a walk. i'm back at 4:30ish; mom still moanin' and groanin'. now she's yelling, "i'm floating." donna's holding her hand, calming her down. she's getting a breathing treatment. 6:30 p.m. mom wakes up crying and moaning. "oh oui, it hurts, it hurts, it hurts." donna holds her hand; calms her down and talks gently to her. mom just had the morphine under the tongue. donna thinks there will be no tomorrow when i ask how we'll divide the day. i think i'll stay till 9 or so tonight; i sure would hate for mom to die alone, but it seems we always think she's dying and she doesn't. 7:15 p.m. mom sleeps a bit, then starts her moaning and groaning. we adjust her legs, her feet. mom has those "dead eyes" again, they're open but have a far-away look. oh, mom. god bless you. you don't deserve all this. god, please, take mom. please take her. i don't know what to do. stay all night, again? stay? get some sleep, at donna's? i don't know when mom's going. if she's going. oh, mom.

April 6, 2003

i'm writing at 5 p.m. trying to remember. we left after 8 p.m. last night. mom was resting, had her morphine, nurses all around. we were encouraged by the nurse to go. it was hard to leave, but i'm sure we look like zombies. i'd hate to have mom die without us there. after all this. but, we went. the clocks sprung ahead; it's not that we slept in, but we were both up after 7; which is really late for us. donna got dressed and raced over; i walked for twenty minutes and was to call donna. she called me; "mom doesn't look good. breathing questionable." i was ready. came over in a flash; was in mom's room before 8. we've been bedside ever since; mom still here, albeit a very weakened state. she's not acknowledged us today; in another place. her eyes are open, but have that "i'm not here look" to them. there was one audible statement at 11ish; "i'm dying." there's been nothing but mumbles, moans, groans, and the odd, loud scream. we've pretty well kept to her morphine schedule for pain. lynne, the respiratory therapist, put the finger monitor on; oxygen level very low. oh mom; so sorry you are suffering. why aren't you long gone? mom's nurse is off the floor; we're asking for morphine every hour now as dr. wenzke ok'd that if needed—if mom wasn't comfortable. and boy, she's not. donna and i have been here over nine hours now, donna a bit longer. we've finally turned the war on tv on; no sound. we've been totally focused on mom, and yet, she's not passing, once again. i can't believe it.

strangely enough, she really isn't here, either. spooky. now it's 9 p.m. and donna and i are thinking this is the night. we'll stay. all night? for a while? until? now mom is breathing a bit more regularly. my god, this is something else. mom has the oxygen mask on, morphine every hour, she's pretty quiet. i bet she'll last through the night. oh shit, the nurse was just in, mom's oxygen intake is very low and her feet are discolored. her arm (left) and hands swollen. they have been for a bit but seem to be getting larger. she's not going to make it. not much longer. we have "anaconda" on. no sound. how stupid is this movie? love being with mom, but need relief. there is none. yes, there is. this stupid movie. the relief is death. oh mom, i wish there could be a miracle. you die or awake totally healthy. or you be at peace. you and god decide. this no-man's-land sucks. ron's been here a lot; off and on; nancy's been here. mom is loved. her sister, aunt barb, has called. cousin kerin called. i keep going to mom, stroking her face gently, telling her to go in peace, telling her how much we love her. telling her how many people love her. encourage her not to be afraid. telling her i think it's going to be beautiful; she'll see dad, a lot of her sisters and brothers. the nurse is in; she thinks mom has a bluish color to her. i don't see it. selective vision, who knows? she's here; then she'll be gone. profound. it'll be a moment. honestly, it'll be something. it's almost 11 p.m. mom still breathing. we're so tired. the nurse comes in and says, "in my honest opinion, go. i think she'll hold on. and sometimes they don't want anyone around when they die." oh god, these are agonizing decisions . . . go, stay? well, i'm embarrassed to say, we're going. it didn't take too much encouragement for us to leave. oh mom . . . go in peace . . . whether we're here or not. if you want to die alone, do it. god bless you, mom. i love you, mom. this is so sad; so fucking sad.

April 7, 2003

it was good to get some sleep. i'm happy mom is still here. we returned 7:30 a.m. we talk to mom, who's in another world. coma-like. sad to see. mom's breathing is heavy now; the regular nursing staff all on duty and everyone shocked to see mom's still alive. every time they go home, it's like the last good-bye. everyone's being sensitive, kind, caring, compassionate. it's around 8:30 now; dr. wenzke came in. "shouldn't be long, now." he reviews the orders. mom's feet are blue, i almost can't look at them. her eyes are only slits. god bless you, mom. this is horrible. i sure hope you aren't in pain. it's between mom and god now. i'm saying the rosary, continually. donna had a dead gingko leaf on her shoe; quite beautiful. for some reason, it stuck to her shoe. gingko—the tree of life. this flawed, beautiful dead leaf; i'm keeping it. symbolic. reminds me of something funny last night; i'm poetically saying how mom's dead eyes still search for the portal to the mystery. donna looks at nancy and says "she's poetic . . . but it's the morphine!" we all laughed. it was one of those "in the moment" things. 9:45 a.m. very quiet. donna and i are reading bible passages to mom; it's nice. just changed my phone message (again); gone two weeks today. left a message for caroline. don't think it'll be long now. then off to arizona. can't even think about it. 10:15 . . . darlene comes in with mom's hourly dose. mom has deep convulsive breathes; hard to watch. just read an awful article on the coming extinction of gorillas and chimps. poachers and ebola. what a tragedy. what sadness. you look at the gorgeous, beautiful faces of chimps and gorillas; look into those eyes. oh, my god. so beautiful. so human. so full of soul. how can we let this happen; disease terrible enough, but poachers? who's paying the poachers? that's the crime! how can we ever right this world? that's a question that should be asked every day. every day. each person do one thing to right the world. not much to ask. there's gotta be a way. gotta be. 1:45 p.m. we've eaten. ron brought in chili, nancy's still here, the staff keep coming in. both marys just rolled mom; we left the room. mom had no response to them. she's really gone. pastor paul was just in with tracey; we had a nice prayer. nancy was telling pastor paul a beautiful story. elizabeth was being cared for by a friend of nancy's. elizabeth asked if al (my dad) would have flowers waiting for gigi (grandma). the friend said, "i'm sure he will." elizabeth continues on about maybe flowers are hard to find in heaven. it's been a long time. maybe that's why gigi is still here. elizabeth then said, "maybe flowers would make my mama feel better" and nance's friend replied, "probably." then elizabeth walked over to the $29.95 roses and nance's friend said, "well, your mother probably doesn't feel that bad." they wound up with carnations. sweet elizabeth. mom looks bad. mouth wide open, the bag on her breathing mask is full, puffed out. reminds me when i had my temporary colostomy after passing gas. freaky. bad memories. another shot. another hour. oh mom. you or god, someone let go here. taking a break. i think it's 4 p.m. a few tears here and there. i cry about missing home as much as missing mom; she's gone already, really she is. has that labored breathing; gasping, heavy deep breaths, from an empty body, the talkative, loving, little girl personality silenced. darlene, i think, put a call in to the doctor about "this shot, a shot" to help with mom's labored breathing. now ann is on and putting in another call. maybe it would be a mercy shot. but, i don't think so. in a way, i can see why one would do that. it's ok to do, in a case like this. but then, is it god's call? or is there really a god? does he, she have a phone? line busy? constantly? i'm so overtired. confused. ron and nancy went off on an errand. donna and i tend to mom; but no tending. just witnessing. praying. loving. the war in iraq is on. all kinds of battles; here and there. no weapons of mass destruction. makes you wonder. no news of the proposed department of peace, anywhere. makes you wonder. that should be front page, for christ's sake. i've faxed, phoned, and e-mailed friends about supporting it. that's all one can do. support the good stuff. but support means do something. i'm thinking about who i call when mom passes. poor mom has a fever of 103. not good. could this woman have any other friggin' challenge? oh mom. i'm so sorry. jesus. kesha just in; she's been very kind. taking mom's temp again. it's about 5:30 now. they've given mom a tylenol suppository. we've cold clothed her for about fifteen minutes. i think the fever is coming down; at least she seems cooler. they say some get a fever before passing. oh, mom. i love you so much. i shut mom's slits; those damn open slits of eyes. so weird. i stroked the cold cloth over them. they did close. she looks better with her eyes closed. damn, they've opened again. what the hell? held mom's hand for about ten minutes, praying for god to take mom. thy will be done. please. soon. please go, mom; while donna and i are here. we want to be with you. i think it would be a damn shame to die alone. for anyone. but mom, not you. please don't. we're waiting for ron to bring us cocktails. then donna and ron will go to the cafe for a quick dinner. it's a cold wintery day. bleak outside. i'm glad we're in this room. big window. an extension to the room; an extension of life, for thoughts. i wonder if mom is choosing a day, this day? is there a choice? i'm feeling so unhappy right now. i am unhappy. i guess someday i'll understand. why can't we understand on this side??? this is a situation where one is powerless. the mystery of death is baffling to me. when you finally have your nose in it, it's baffling. not that pretty. just going to be with mom. oh, mom. i love you so much. so much. it's a bit later. ron left. donna and i still here. we're beat. i'm encouraging donna to go home. she's exhausted. looks like shit. i say, "you look like i feel." we laugh. we're settling into those damn uncomfortable chairs. at one point donna repeats her famous line, after a great struggle between stay and go; " if mom's not dead by 9, i'm leaving." for some reason, and i have no idea why, i'm into staying. "i'll watch tv. hold mom's hand. i'll come home later." for some reason, i wanted to stay.

April 8, 2003

mom passed at 12:32 a.m. i looked at my watch. it's strange looking at her now; waiting for the mortician to come and take her out of the room. donna and ron already left with the room's contents. i just don't want to leave mom alone. it doesn't feel right. i was here, alone, with mom, watching tv. holding her hand. her breathing just slowed; slowed noticeably. i immediately called for the nurses, "is this it? is this what happens?" the nurse nodded her head, yes. "please, call my sister!" i started stroking mom's head; "go in peace mom, go in peace. i love you so much. go in peace mom. you're not alone. love you, mom." of course, i was crying but trying to keep it together. then, a few short puffs. then nothing. no breathing. nothing. i couldn't believe the immediate change. it's like mom's spirit took off, fast. just got the hell out of there. i felt no presence of soul energy, no presence of anything. an empty shell. mom looked different; all of a sudden, she looked different, so unlike my mom. i kept stroking her face, holding her hand. "go in peace mama, go in peace." then i said things like, "this was such a privilege, mom, such a privilege to be here with you. to witness your going. oh, mom . . . i love you so much." i felt it such a privilege to sit with her body; this damn body that wouldn't give in. i started to think how at peace she must be . . . but where was she, already? heaven? on her way? was she watching me? i felt she was so far away. she got outta there like a bat out of hell. what an expression that is! you know what i mean. she exited fast. it was strange to see mom; no masks, no labored breathing, just dead. dead. a dead body. i thought i'd be afraid, but i wasn't. i actually sat on the bed. just stroked that dead body. the room wasn't spooky, either. there was peace. it's mind-boggling. nurses do wash the dead body. i watched that. strange. i guess i ought to pee and be ready to leave when they take mom. oh, mom, i love you so. where are you? it's almost 2:30 a.m. they've come for you mom. i can't watch this. there's a bag. you'll be in it. it'll be zipped shut. i can't watch that mom. i hate to leave you. i miss you so much already. the guy is dave, mom. from walker funeral home. he'll be gentle, i made him promise. my last good-bye to your dead body. mom, you don't look like mom. wherever you are, mom, you were so strong, courageous. you gave us all so much. so much good, mom. god bless this dead body. safe journey to arizona. see you there. love you, mom. god bless. god bless you, mom. wherever you are. thank you, again, for letting me be here. i know you're a private person, really. thank you, mom. i left crying. feeling numb. my god, it's over. as i drove back to donna and ron's i was stunned. stunned. mom's gone. i went over the events of this last day and evening and night. thank god i was there. it just couldn't be any other way. mom, oh mom. god bless you. i miss you already, mom. i do. i cried and cried. i wish she could tell me about what's up, now. try me, mom. tell me. talk to me. darn it. i hear nothing. i see nothing. i shouldn't be driving. i'm crying too much. thank god it's a short distance. i'm stunned. mom's gone. gone home. how nice that must be. no place like home. i miss you, mom. when i got to donna and ron's, they were still up. in the living room. belting a few back. donna had all these lists going, things to do. oh, my god. i couldn't believe it. so organized. hell, things had to be done. it was death energy, sad energy. i was spent. suggested we continue in the morning. brain dead. my sister and i are both morning people; in that respect we take after dad. he could get up so damn early and just be. be with himself, the birds, the morning sky, the quiet. donna and i are like that. we're also overachievers in the a.m. we function! damn, i couldn't sleep. i was doing e-mails till 4 a.m. up at 7 a.m. i think i cried from 4 to 7. donna had already e-mailed the entire family by the time i got up. we were on our way to a day filled with the business of death. walkers, the funeral home in toledo, was making the arrangements for mom to travel to arizona. we gathered the obit material we had done before; that part was fairly organized. a good suggestion for everyone; have that obit written. that's a good thing to get out of the way. we had to get our airline tickets organized. the errands, errands, errands. fax obits, stop by lake park, thank-you cards, stop by kingston and tell them. donna and ron went to mom's lock-up to get a few things for the viewing in arizona. things we'd forgotten. did i have the right clothes? need anything? you run around, not like a chicken with your head cut off, but run. it was definitely on death energy. shock energy. then, final packing and things like mom's glasses, a rosary, jewelry she'll wear at the viewing. honestly, it was a day. to bed and setting the clock for some un-godly hour for the flight to arizona. we were leaving the house at 4:30 a.m.

April 9, 2003

finally, arizona. we were on our flight at 6:10 a.m. wondering if mom's flight was ok, wondering if she knew she was home. going into mom's house . . . without mom being there . . . looking at everything with dead eyes now. it was weird. how i miss mom. have a lot to do. i think it's wednesday. with the time difference and all, i'm so out of it. i think we put our luggage down, ron gets the car to work, and we're off to the funeral home. lots to do. there is a business to death. thank god we've got a committee. mom had ordered her casket and paid for her funeral long ago. the casket she ordered is no longer in stock. the funeral director at menke's showed us a substitute, near the price but an upgrade, that he thought we'd like. we didn't. it was a bit too fancy. the embroidery was not mom. we settled on something we felt mom would enjoy lying in. a bit weird. my first casket experience. then we picked flowers for mom; for on the casket and mom's corsage. it must be a gardenia . . . mom's favorite. the spray for the casket; carnations were ok. ribbon wording? details. details. details. planned the visitation and rosary. the drive by the house, before mass. mom's wish will be honored. so nice. then, cemetery papers, we have to go there. there are mausoleum papers. need to go to the church office about the mass, the priest, what the priest says about mom. then grab lunch. then home to create more lists . . . more tasks . . . clean. no one's really been in the house for a year. nick comes and goes; does his laundry, airs it out; runs the odd vacuum, and dust cloth. no one is here, so nothing needed to be done inside. we've had the yard work kept up with. actually; inside and out looks good. mom would be happy. she wanted to come back. god bless her. calling people. come to the visitation, the mass, come over after. so much to do. visit dear old friends ed and alice; our old neighbors from hillside, illinois, days. drink too much. get into family flares. oh, well. walk away. breathe. caroline's coming. so great. stan too, but when? where is he? so much to remember. clean the place. shopping. get organized for friday. killer day ahead, preparing. mom's viewing on friday is 4 to 6 or something like that. with the rosary at the end. then out to dinner. stan coming friday. caroline coming friday night. donna and ron will shop friday a.m. for after the mass reception on saturday. i'll clean. we're on top of the plans. i think we're in bed by 9 p.m., but again, i can't sleep. i'm so wound up with death business and busy-ness. missing mom. i'll just write in my diary. mom's diary. i can't wait for peace and quiet. it seems so long since i've had it. i need solitude to live. i do. very monk-like. i need time and quiet for my grieving. this is autopilot. demanding. i am remembering how i cried at the church office; some guy from st. vincent de paul society, on the phone, was talking to me regarding how they all loved mom. they're giving her a brick in the memorial garden in phoenix. a gesture to honor all of her years of volunteering. i'm touched, i'm bawling. my sister doesn't get it as deeply as i do. or she's more controlled. i lose it. i'm so proud of mom; so naked. so happy, so proud. the society was her life . . . her volunteering gave her a sense of value, identity. sense of purpose. my god, don't we all need that! i've got to see that brick! so proud of you mom. so proud.

April 10, 2003

early morning, i'm crying again. this is how overtired one can get and lose perspective. i realize i overlooked caroline in the family recognition. i feel badly. i didn't put caroline's name in the obit. you know how they have a name in parentheses . . . like donna boehme (roycht) or nancy rasky (boehme). an identification thing . . . well . . . i had nothing that indicated caroline was my partner for these past twenty some odd years. i felt badly. i mean, she shared all my emotional journeys about mom. supported me totally about whatever i needed regarding mom. was just there. totally, however needed. she's part of my life! i didn't acknowledge her. i felt so badly. i really felt i did a grave disservice. i think i was questioned at the funeral parlor about it. i wasn't thinking. caroline, cut out. not only of my life, but mom's life. she was a part of mom's life too. so, this morning, while writing this entry, i feel disappointed in myself. a grave error in decision making. i wasn't thinking. brain dead. it's like a few years back i noticed on mom's shelves, where all the family pictures were, no pictures of caroline and me, our dogs, or our cat. pictures of everyone else. lots of pictures of me with the family, but none of caroline, me, our family. so i started sending these pictures and up they went. it's just doing it. noticing things and correcting them. you want to be included . . . include yourself! and your partner, your family, whatever. it was all such a wake-up call. those calls never stop coming, by the way. express yourself. a mistake is made, correct it. move on. get with the program. it's that easy. my idea is caroline is included in the family and that's what she is when the family takes the water and wine down to the priest at the mass. yes, that's exactly what should happen! i share this with donna as soon as she's up. she's totally fine with that. it's ron, donna, me, caroline, and nick with the offering. the family! oh, god. everything is a friggin' process. this whole death business has a speed, and brother, it's fast. i'm so overtired. want to write more but i think i'll just shut my eyes a moment and breathe. oh, mom. how i hope you're watching all this. it's all for you. we're honoring you. we love you. feel it, mom. hope you are feeling it. i took a long break from writing. it's been a day. i was cleaning for a lot of it. radio on, volume up. healing. we're all overtired but good. you just go. just do. i went through mom's closet and was wearing a blue top of hers. it's a medium and i'm not a medium. i just wanted to wear something of mom's. i kept looking at this one picture of mom, smiling. looked so happy. that's how i picture mom. there's a dove on the front porch; made a nest by the door on a planter. i'm calling the dove catherine. ron flew the american flag at half-mast. mom and dad have a flag pole in their front yard. donna and ron shopped for the party on saturday. did good. after lunch i went to the mall. one last look around for anything to make me look good for mom. i was going through viewing and funeral panic. got two new pairs of birkenstocks. one blue, one black. nice. not the klondike dyke-things. donna needed nylons. ron made dinner. lots of friends and family phoned. caroline's in a panic. she was in the midst of renewing her dutch passport and all papers are in ottawa. she needs her passport for arizona. so she's trying to get her papers. it's a nail-biter. she's booked on a hundred different flights. in the hands of god. dear neighbors jack and rita were over. there was laughter. nice to hear. i just had wine with dinner. that felt good. nick came for dinner. we were all so tired. went to bed at 9:30. couldn't sleep. so overtired. so wrote down everything i could remember for this day. now i've got to try to sleep!

April 11, 2003

couldn't sleep. meditated, prayed, up about 6. donna's already up, but going back to bed. i talked with caroline; she's coming! oh, that's good. will be here tonight. donna, ron and i do our morning walk. i go off to church. it's good to move. changes that sorrowful energy. the priest calls; father dion, so nice, he knew mom. he came to wish her well before she left for toledo. he was good to her, kind. he'll do well. we go to cathy's across the street; start hauling plants and flowers over. she always has so many. we're designating her director of flowers and decoration. donna and ron leave to pick up the food for tomorrow and a new flag for mom's house. the one flying now is too tattered. much like mom was. god bless her. i wash the outdoor chairs. no end to the preparation. iron my outfit. take a shower. it's going to happen. the business of death is ready for showtime. pre-prep is over. the show's about to "go to camera." somewhere in this mad morning donna, ron and i run over to see mom, how she looks. final check. i touch her hand and kiss her forehead. so hard already. she doesn't look like mom. i remember touching dad in his coffin; he was so hard too. i hate that. i guess mom looks good. to me, artificial. i'm doing ok. i'm half faking it, half ok. i think we're all in that boat. i still feel mom's spirit is long gone. i see mom as that happy woman, smiling and laughing in the one collage i made of the family way back in '85. that's how she is now. in my memory. donna, ron, and stan come in the door with all the food and groceries. stan got here early this a.m. he's staying at some motel near us. he likes his privacy. it's good to see him. donna and ron pick him up on the way back from the commissary; where they shop. we're going to eat and get ready for the viewing. i think i'm ready. hang on, mom. the show's about to begin.

April 13, 2003

well, it came and went. it was fast and furious. many people, many stories, much going on. mom would be proud. everything was beautiful; especially the mass. what father dion said about mom was perfect. he really did outline her challenged life from the farm, to the move out here, and everything in between. he mentioned all her involvements. she was a mover and shaker, with all the volunteer work, especially after dad died. she blossomed for several years. things changed as her health started a downhill decline. over time, volunteering wasn't as much a priority as it was a challenge. she was ill for a few years; she was. perhaps we left her too long. you let them live. you let them live in their worlds, don't you? there's never a good time to say "you're becoming toast. big changes to come." well, that's what happens, isn't it? so heart-wrenching when one has to change their life. i know how i feel about change at this age; it must be hell for older people. it was for mom. i know it was. the gathering at the house, after mass, was very nice. all the neighbors and friends. we did have a house full. you hear stories, have fun, laugh. share all the memories you have and then more are added. the st. vincent de paul people couldn't say enough. and yes, she's brick number 208 in the garden; their memorial garden. i can't wait to see it. i'll have lunch and sit in that garden . . . more than once! a deacon said the rosary after friday's viewing. that was nice. he gave us the new "finger" rosaries. we went to tivoli gardens after the friday affair. thought we'd be home in time for caroline, but she beat us. was waiting in the dark, on the back patio. i felt badly we weren't home for her arrival. it was comforting to have her come; and stan to be with us. we visited and yakked and laughed and cried. a family friend came over friday night with a cake for saturday; sat and drank. i had to go to bed, i was tired. caroline and i slept in the same bed; which we haven't done for years. and a double bed! we're both used to our queen-size beds! disastrous. neither one of us slept. i find it funny that anyone accuses someone of snoring, because usually the accusor also snores. caroline's a mover in bed. we're both light sleepers. it was disastrous. up bright and early, nick gets stan. we all leave in time, to get to mom's, the church. cathy finishes with the flowers. the house looks lived in, nice. we get to menkes' after a bit of confusion on the road; nick is sensitive too, and sad. we catch a freight train at the crossing; had to wait. we say good-bye to mom before the casket is shut and off to mass. ken, from menke's, takes off all the jewelry. that's sad, too. we follow mom in the hearse, first to her home for a drive by . . . her good-bye . . . which she wanted so badly. one last moment. then to church, the mass, the sermon, and then, everyone back to the house. oh mama, it was perfect. your favorite music in church, all the things you wanted, so many dear friends, so much love and admiration for you. you would have loved it. you must have loved it. after church, taking you to your new home, sunland mausoleum. short service there. my god, mausoleums smell. they smell of the dead. some strange aroma. i hate that smell. and they have a fly catcher that zaps things in the air. it makes a zapping noise . . . cause it's arizona and things fly around. little things. it's bizarre, from my point of view. there you are mom, with dad. i think he's in first, then you. so many bodies in this wall, hall, the place. this is what you and dad wanted. god bless you, mom. it's over now. the entire journey, from birth to death, to rest. for the body, it's over. now we deal with your absence. the love in our hearts, the memories. donna, as executor of the will, will have some work to do. too early for any thoughts, decisions. my only thought is i'm happy i spent so much time with you. i loved our more intimate moments and sharing so much, mom. i'm sorry you couldn't die at home, mom. we really wanted that to happen. you got so sick in the end, so quickly, there was no way to travel. really. we did our very best mom, for you. you know that. the love, appreciation, admiration . . . will go on forever. love you, mom. i'll return to crestbrook, i'll visit you at sunland. you're in my heart, on my mind, you're a part of me. you'll live forever in this diary. my god, what a journey, mom. damn, you were courageous. i'm sorry you suffered. god bless you, mother. god bless you. enjoy where you are. and don't forget, you be my angel. how lucky am i! love you. love you, mom.

April 21, 2003

easter monday. feels quiet; is quiet. so so so good to be home. a long walk on the beach today with the dogs. errands. gassed up the car, did some banking at the machine. have a tight schedule today; working for rita and ingie. taking them to the airport and dropping off their dog, jessie, at their friend's. will start to get my life in order. i'm taking at least two weeks to get organized and just "be." i realized at donna's, upon returning, i just haven't had a moment to really feel the impact. the emptiness. the void. i usually process later. after something. i need to go slow, be quiet, be alone. just hear god. mom. peace. hear them, hear it. slowly catch up with my life. it feels, now that i am home and have me back, that it's been a long haul. it has. the entire year. as soon as mom arrived in toledo . . . the following week, it was pneumonia. thus far this year, i've spent two months with mom, donna, and ron. slightly more time with them than with my own family. i do have to take time to put me, my life, in order. i miss mom. oh yeah. i can feel it. but i have peace. i really do. i just feel sad. i'm tired too; not so much physically. physically, i can't wait to get moving. get in better shape. drop a few pounds. i ate and drank a fair bit this last year; emotional fill up. not good. i'm good with discipline, so i'll be all right. am going to join weight watchers. i'm a group gal. that'll work. i think it's healthy to think in terms of smaller amounts. period. move more, eat less. eat right. that's the diet of reality.

process feeling in a healthy way. time. taking time is healthy. being quiet, for me, is healthy. praying, churches of my mood, writing poetry regarding my feelings. all that. i need time. balancing people, places, things in my life. it'll take time. i've got to be good to me. i will. it's a blur . . . since i drove caroline to the airport a week ago sunday, in sun city. a blur. i think we went to the lawyer on monday. then it was a marathon. lots of time with the lawyer, seeing a few close friends, thank-you cards; just things about mom's death. donna is the executor of the will, but since mom divided everything equally, we were both at the lawyers all the time. neither one of us slept well, up very early each day. at midnight friday we were on the plane to toledo. saturday a busy day there, but i was wise enough to book and get a massage for myself, as everything ached. poor donna; stuck with the paperwork, the locker, the legal shit. donna and ron need their life back, too. it's good. we're all back, will have our lives. donna will get a system together, stay on top of things. i went to easter service in warren, with marianne. i was happy to be there, but needed to come home. only stayed for one service. no energy. i'm glad i went, marianne's talk was so damn good, and clear, about the meaning of easter. dwell on the resurrection not the crucifixion, in our lives. my god, the woman is brilliant. that talk should be heard by every person on the planet. it was so inspirational. motivating. i'm ready. get this diary written and published. get the weight off and be in good physical shape. love. just love. be and use my intelligence. be the best i can be, in all ways. damn it. i'm going to do that. i've pretty well been on that road; my life, self-esteem and love for self; all good. one can get lazy. caution. mom will help motivate me. that's a good use of my feelings and love. the new train, that i'm catching, is the 208. marianne has a lecture on a tape i have. it's about how we're at the train station but often waiting for the wrong train. we don't get on the right train. that's why things don't go well. 208 is mom's memorial brick in the st. vincent de paul garden, in phoenix. for volunteer service above and beyond the call of duty. i'm damn proud of mom. with the cards she was dealt, she was so amazing; who she was, what she did, what she accomplished, how good she was with money, and for her courage and spirit the last year of her life. mom, you blow me away. you do. love you. love you. so, that's it. my last entry. mom died. mom has risen. mom will come again; in thoughts, memories, motivational moments. i'll see her as the engineer on the 208. there are certain pictures of her with that beautiful smile. that's the picture in my mind's eye and heart. it will keep me smiling. i'm at the train station and yippee, here comes the 208! it's the right train for me. the "do my best in life" train. yep. the right train for me. mom, i learned so much this past year. thank you. i was taken many places, met many people. thank you. most of all, i got to know you well. you're the best, mom. the very best. love you to bits! so, reader. i do hope this diary helps you in some way. it sure helped me. god bless you and your process with your loved ones. your process with your life. remember, it's a new day. be your best!!! i'm off now. done. you're on your own. you can do it!

Order Information

To order copies of *If Mom's Not Dead by 9, I'm Leaving* for a loved one or a friend, please contact Charoy Publishing:

Telephone: 416-691-5459
Fax: 416-691-0155
E-Mail: charoy@interlog.com
Web site: www.roycht.com

Purchasing Information:
$24.50 Canadian / $18.50 U.S. / $15.00 Euro
plus 7% Ontario sales tax

Mailing Information for single copies:
add $2.40 for shipping within Canada (2 to 4 days)
add $5.60 for shipping to the U.S. (4 to 6 days)
add $11.50 for shipping to Europe (2 weeks)

Send check or money order made payable to: Charlene Roycht

Prices subject to change.

The author is available to speak at seminars, and for personal coaching, poetry readings, and consulting. Please contact Charlene Roycht at:

Charoy Publishing
Box 101
2192 Queen St., East
Toronto, Ontario M4E 1E6
Telephone: 416-691-5459